*a guide to m*
*sixties* *the be*

# 60
## making
### *the* **most** *of* **it**

# RICHARD JACKSON

# RETHINK PRESS

First published in Great Britain 2014
by Rethink Press (www.rethinkpress.com)

Cover image © James Weston

# CONTENTS

*Dedicated to my mother and father.*

# PREFACE

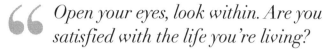 *Open your eyes, look within. Are you satisfied with the life you're living?*

Bob Marley

As I approached my sixtieth birthday I had absolutely no thoughts about writing a book focussed on that landmark event. Nor had I even considered putting into words how I would go about ensuring that my life was lived to the full in the following years.

I was in a fortunate position that I had already retired after over forty years of work but I was also aware that I would have a lot of time to fill without the daily routine of work.

I already felt motivated to tackle this problem head on and to make sure that my new found time was filled with doing things and enjoying life as much as I could. My motivation was to a large extent driven by memories of my father who had always looked forward to his retirement, but sadly never made it as he was struck down by illness and died when he was just fifty-six.

Most of my life had been spent living in the same area of England and I had grown up with people who were still friends and with whom I would meet from time to time. Each had their own story to tell about how their life had worked out and where they had ended up by the time they had reached sixty. Knowing these people and observing them as they grew older, gradually made a deep impression on me and my thoughts about reaching this notable age.

What struck me was their tremendous diversity of attitude regarding their futures and what they were going to do with the rest of their lives. Some were already very well organised and had established plans that they were pursuing. Others had only negative thoughts about life after sixty and were taking it a day at a time with no planning and little attempt to make sure that not a day was wasted.

There were also other noticeable differences between them. Some were very fit; looked in great shape and looked younger than their actual years. Others had not done so well and were out of shape; suffered from ailments and looked older than they actually were. The differences were very noticeable in the physical sense and from conversations there was a further marked difference. Those who had looked after themselves well, seemed energised and alive with hope and expectation. There was a real buzz to their personality.

Those who had not looked after themselves so well sometimes seemed slightly defeated and had resigned themselves to old age and a life of complacency. You could almost sense an air of defeat and acceptance about how they felt about themselves and their futures.

These observations inspired me to think even deeper about my own attitude to reaching sixty and what I was going to do with the rest of my life. I even searched out books that were based on the subject of reaching sixty, but found them, in the main, to be either making a joke of it or written in a very patronising and derogatory manner.

These books were of little or no use so I decided that I needed to find my own answers. I knew that I was in reasonable shape physically, was reasonably sound financially and had a number of good and close relationships. There remained however, a desire to do a lot more with my life while I was still willing and able. It was not a question of being discontent or dissatisfied with how things were but more a feeling of things that had not yet been done and could still be achieved. Perhaps it could be described as a real desire to live the rest of my life to the full.

They say that time waits for no man; there would never be another chance if I missed out this time.

I realised that I could only do everything I wanted and feel really fulfilled, if I got myself organised and planned all the aspects of my life that I thought were important. So that is exactly what I did and continue to do so right up to the present time. I filled page after page with my thoughts and plans until I reached the point, at which I needed to start doing things, rather than just thinking about them.

Since I started doing so I can truly say that my life has been full of activity and pleasure. Sometimes I may feel over organised and short of time but that is exactly how I like it rather than having spare time on my hands and feeling bored. It may feel exhausting sometimes but it is rewarding and fulfilling with plenty more still to look forward to.

I can understand that some people may reach sixty and have

a different perspective on their futures. They may feel that after a lifetime of work they would like to be less well organised and have a great deal more spare time. Time to relax and do what they want to do, when they want to do it. We are all different so we will all have different needs and desires and that should be respected.

Everybody is free to make their own choices but I would suggest that there is a note of caution that everyone should bear in mind.

Time passes quickly after sixty and the years can slip by almost unnoticed and as this happens you may become less and less inclined to do something different in your life. Energy levels will be in decline and the desire to step outside your comfortable existence will be rapidly waning.

This book is about sharing my own thoughts and feelings on maximising life from sixty onwards, with the intention of making it a busy, happy and rewarding time. It is up to you whether or not you take that on board for yourself.

However, in sharing them with you, I hope that you can benefit from some of my ideas, which could be added to yours to make your own life equally rewarding and fulfilling.

As you will probably already be aware, one of the first things to go wrong as we get older is that our short term memory begins to deteriorate. With this in mind you will find, at the end of each chapter, a few reminders of key points from within that chapter. This will help you to refer back to useful information without having to read the whole chapter again.

Good Luck for the Future and Make the Most of It!

# INTRODUCTION

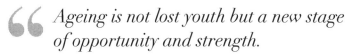 *Ageing is not lost youth but a new stage of opportunity and strength.*

Betty Friedan

## No-one lives forever

There is no truer statement of fact, or a better known certainty, than no-one lives forever. We can take that as a solid fact that has truly stood the test of time. No matter how hard anyone has tried (and many have!) to buck the trend, they have inevitably failed.

During our lives, however, we can sometimes be tempted into making the mistake of thinking that we will live forever and that somehow we will be the one who is able to buck the trend and live in perpetuity. It is a common mistake, made by many, because facing our own ultimate mortality can be a painful and unpleasant task that we can understandably and easily choose to ignore. It is a natural defence mechanism to allow our brains to block out unpleasant thoughts. Rather like other unpleasant things in our lives, we hope that by ignoring it, we can make ourselves believe that it will go away and never happen.

Many people make this foolish mistake and with such a mental approach it is easy to fall into the trap of thinking that

1

there is plenty of time to do and achieve everything. 'There's no hurry, there's plenty of time left!'

## Tomorrow Never Comes!

Waiting often turns out to be a big mistake as tomorrow never comes. Missing out on your desires and ambitions while you can still enjoy them is rather like going on the holiday of a lifetime and then staying in your hotel room when you get there. Instead of enjoying yourself and making the most of your holiday you miss out on all the fabulous things you could have done while you had the chance.

You would be unlikely to be as stupid as that, and would take the opportunity to enjoy as much as you could while you had that chance! You would make sure that you made the most of your precious time and the hard earned money you had spent getting there.

So why do some of us make the same mistake with our lives while we are living them and still have the opportunity to make the most of the time we have? As you will know, you only get one chance to live your life so why not use every minute of it to your fullest advantage.

## It's Time to Live Life to the Full

When you reach the age of sixty, statistics indicate that you still have (getting on for) 30% of your life in front of you. Time, during which you may not be working as hard as you used to, or bringing up a family, and will have more time to think about what you want to do and the chance to get on and do it.

This has to be fantastic and very welcome news! Life is definitely not over when you reach sixty. In fact, it should be the beginning of an exciting and enjoyable new phase of your life. It should be **your** time when you can indulge yourself rather than doing what everybody else would have you do. At sixty there's a lot of living still to do and the chance to fill that time with fulfilling experiences and enjoyment.

If you are about to reach the age of sixty (or have already got there) the question to ask yourself has to be…

**What are you waiting for?**

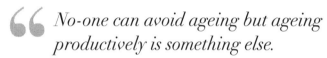 *No-one can avoid ageing but ageing productively is something else.*

Katharine Graham

---
## MEMORY JOGGERS

- ◎ Remember that we are all mortal, even you, and you will definitely not live forever.
- ◎ Use every minute you have to live your life to the full.
- ◎ When you reach sixty, statistics indicate that you still have, on average, 30% of your life ahead of you.

# 1.

## PERCEPTIONS OF REACHING SIXTY

 *You know you're getting old when all the names in your black book have M.D. after them.*

Harrison Ford

Listening to the radio, you may have often heard dedications being played to celebrate special events in people's lives. From weddings to anniversaries; births to birthdays and sometimes just to mark a special occasion.

Frequently there are dedications being played for people's landmark birthdays such as someone about to celebrate their sixtieth birthday. Nothing wrong with that you might think and you are absolutely right. Requesting a song for a loved one on the radio is certainly a good way of showing the world how much you care for that person.

You may have also noticed that when this happens the Presenter frequently uses phrases that provoke special attention from the listening audience. These whimsical phrases often reflect a way of negative thinking associated with age that we should challenge, at least in our own minds and perhaps as a generation in general.

'You've reached the Big Sixty. Never mind, it's only a number,' is an example of how they often round off the request and, of course, there is a major emphasis on the word 'Big' in the way they pronounce it. There may even be a slight hint of a chuckle as well in the way they say 'Never mind'.

If you are the 'lucky' recipient of such a dedication you may, as a result, be experiencing mixed emotions after hearing it. Joy mixed with apprehension; pleasure but also concern; happy but slightly sad as well.

In fact we could all be left wondering what less than positive thoughts are being etched into the mind of not only the particular person who's birthday it is, but also in the minds of all those who are either approaching the 'Big Sixty' or have already arrived.

Firstly, in describing sixty as 'Big', it could be taken to imply that it is a considerably large number of years for anyone to reach which in turn, would infer, that it is at the wrong end of the age spectrum.

Secondly, in referring to this milestone in this particular way, the radio presenter is attempting to offer mitigation to the unfortunate person on reaching that age by indicating that it is only a number and therefore they should not worry about it. However, in doing so, is the presenter really indicating to that individual that they should be worried about reaching sixty? Are they highlighting that the source of that worry was that they were getting old and that old age was an undesirable state?

So although the person had received birthday wishes on the radio station, thanks to the love and thoughtfulness of the individual making the request, did that special moment make them feel full of joy and happiness? Or had the presenter's words simply indicated to them that they were getting old and that it was probably a less than pleasant place to be?

Next time you hear a dedication for a sixtieth birthday on the radio, listen carefully and see how it makes you feel.

After all, when people reach some of the other notable age milestones, the words used to celebrate and congratulate are different to those used for the sixty years milestone.

Take for example the words used when someone reaches the age of twenty-one. Reaching this age is considered cause for celebration using positive terminology to mark the occasion of reaching adulthood with a world of opportunity ahead. 'You've got the key to the door; you've never been twenty-one before!' What a tremendous occasion to celebrate and about which to be happy. The message is totally positive and looks forward to all the opportunities that the future may bring.

Perhaps the next really major landmark birthday is when we reach forty. This is sometimes regarded in a less than positive light as it heralds the onset of middle age, the midlife crisis and all that is associated with it. The changing physical appearance; the endless task of looking after children; the end of sparkling romance as love and relationships mature and the shortness of breath when climbing the stairs, to mention but a few.

However, even with these changes looming on the horizon at forty, there is still plenty of life left in the old dog yet – hence the phrase 'Life begins at forty'. So we can still look at this particular age in a positive way because it is frequently seen as more of a change in the way we approach and live the rest of our lives rather than our life starting to go rapidly into decline. Changes which may come with events such as children becoming more independent; career stability or greater financial security all of which can create greater freedom in life to try new things and experiences.

Even fifty is now seen as the new forty, as life expectancy increases so although it is a landmark which is usually not initially welcomed it is nevertheless an age when there is plenty to look forward to. 'It's nifty to be fifty' nowadays, so get on and enjoy it!

So, the good news is that at the notable ages of twenty-one, forty and even fifty, there is cause not only for celebrating your birthday but also being able to look forward with a degree of positive anticipation and excitement at what life may yet hold for you. Rich and varied experiences yet to come linked to the physical and mental ability to fully enjoy and participate in them. There is, hopefully, plenty good, quality living still to come and also plenty of time (statistically) to enjoy it. Hence, the mind is able to adopt a positive outlook and still be relaxed about how and when these things will happen. Cause for celebration indeed!

So what is it that changes at the age of sixty and why is it viewed by so many in a less positive manner with the emphasis on the 'Big' age?

To find the answer to these questions we need to understand what is going on in our minds and with our belief systems and why we have these beliefs in the first place.

## Do we really believe that we are getting old?

Our belief system is firmly lodged in our sub-conscious mind and is the result of all that we have learnt and experienced throughout our lives from the moment we were born and all of our subsequent experiences.

It can influence and dictate our feelings and emotions as well as the way we behave and react to various stimuli. In the physical sense, for example, we will have learnt, and will therefore believe, that if we put our hand on something hot it will burn us and as a result, cause us pain. In the emotional sense our learnt beliefs will dictate our feelings about such issues as trust and mistrust; what is good and what is bad and the way we should behave.

We will also have learnt from the media, to which we have been exposed, such as: television; the internet; social media; books; newspapers; magazines; radio; and music. Depending on our level of exposure to these different media we will have developed beliefs about all sorts of aspects of life and the world, in which we live. Sometimes these beliefs may be created and fixed in our minds even though they may be inaccurate or not good for us. Unfortunately once established in our minds they are hard to change.

So when it comes to our thoughts about age, and the emotions it creates within us, we already have a belief system which will strongly influence our thoughts and behaviour. In other words our brains have already been hard-wired to react in a certain way.

Naturally, no two people will have been hardwired in

9

exactly the same way or with exactly the same beliefs because everybody has had different experiences and will have grown up in different environments. There will also be a significant change in perspective about the ageing process depending upon the age of the person whose mind is doing the thinking.

For each individual, the way they have been hard-wired when thinking about age and advancing years will have been dependant significantly on two factors. Firstly, there are the opinions and attitudes expressed by persons of significant influence in their own life, such as parents or a teacher, particularly during the person's childhood years. Negative comments about age, made repeatedly by these people, will have lodged firmly in the youngsters mind and stayed there.

Secondly, it will also have been heavily influenced by their own environment as they grew up in what they saw, heard and experienced. An example of this will be your own experiences with older individuals within your family group. Cast your mind back to your own grandparents and conjure up a mental picture of them. Imagine, if you can, how they behaved and acted when you were with them. Did they look very old? Did they behave like an old person? Did others treat them and talk about them like they were old? Your perception of them will have depended on their age at the time and indeed, your own age, but it is likely that they seemed very old to you and this will have helped to build your belief system about age and the way people look and behave as they get older.

Then consider also your own parents, if you can, when they reached the age of sixty. Your perception of them will once again have been influenced by your own age at the time and the way they looked and behaved will have influenced your belief system and will be lodged in your sub-conscious mind. It is likely that these relatives will have created in your mind the model of how you will look and behave when you reach the age of sixty.

Add to this the other experiences you have had in your life involving people who had reached the age of sixty. Maybe this was in the workplace or through friends and acquaintances or even neighbours. Then further add to this what you have seen and read in the various media and you will start to understand how your perception of being sixty has been built and confirmed in your belief system. In other words, how you have been hardwired in your thoughts about being sixty.

## What are your thoughts?

Just stop for a moment and consider your thoughts about reaching the age of sixty? You may have many and you may also realise that each of those thoughts and perceptions is linked to something you have experienced in your own life involving someone who was sixty.

There can be little wonder, then, that our attitudes concerning reaching the age of sixty are so significantly different; it is because we have all had our own experiences of witnessing others at that age.

So if your grandparents and parents at sixty seemed to you to be old and decrepit then your belief will possibly be that everyone, when they reach that age, will also be decrepit. 'Everyone', is also likely to include yourself.

Conversely, however, if they were fit, healthy and highly active at that age then you will naturally expect that everyone can be like that and your own expectations of how you will be at the same age will be influenced accordingly.

## How attitudes have changed

Despite our deep-rooted belief systems, however, something really amazing has happened since the end of the Second World War. Attitudes to growing older have changed and shifted significantly, in keeping with so much else in the world.

The war brought about huge advances in technology which continues to advance at a mind-boggling rate and which have had a huge influence on our lives. But significant social changes have also occurred, with class distinction becoming not only less relevant but unacceptable, while the role of women, within both the family and society in general, has rapidly changed.

So too, have people's attitudes towards how they should lead and enjoy their lives, fuelled initially by a desire to bring an end to the misery of war and austerity. The desire for change created Flower Power and as it swept around the world brought with it freedom of thought and behaviour and an increasingly liberal attitude towards how we should lead our lives. It heralded the beginning of a social revolution, demonstrating that it was no longer necessary or desirable to conform to pre-existing models of behaviour which had dictated the patterns of our lives. In fact to conform was exactly what this new, baby boom generation, did not want to do. It may have seemed shocking at the time but it heralded a wonderful new influence on our belief systems.

With drastically changing attitudes in this generation concerning what they should expect from their lives, there is little wonder that their attitude to age should also have changed from that of their parents and grandparents.

The Swinging Sixties heralded the rise of a generation that wanted pop music, mini-skirts and free love, not food rationing, wars and conscription. This generation wanted to have fun and not be restricted by the codes of previous generations and once they got what they wanted they did not want it to end or stop just there.

Further major cultural change came with the introduction of television as people became increasingly aware of what was happening in the world around them and the exciting challenges and diversity it offered. The stereotyped desire to marry young and start a family, often in their early twenties, was replaced by an even greater desire to enjoy freedom and the delights of the world and to delay settling down in marriage and family life. Thus, couples gradually put off starting a family until much later, and in doing so ensured that they would be much older parents as their children grew up. Having changed the rules established by previous generations governing the way we were expected to behave and think, there was no reason for this new generation not to change their attitudes to ageing as they grew older themselves.

We can see examples of how this has been translated into everyday life all around us in our daily existence. Many of the great Rock Stars of the 1960s and 1970s are still out there performing, some still with their long hair and skinny jeans, despite being well into their sixties. Male or female, they look good, sound great and still wow their fans, many of whom were born long after the 1960s and 1970s.

Neither is it just the pop stars, models or movie stars who are still living their lives to the full and looking and feeling great; it's also many, many men and women of that same generation who are living the same way.

They have decided that they can cast aside pre-conceived ideas and deep rooted beliefs about age and live their lives in a fulfilling, stimulating and exciting way. Still learning and discovering; still participating; still looking forward to the future with anticipation and enthusiasm.

Not for them the pipe and slippers or the twin set and daytime TV, locked into a mundane life offering little excitement and stimulation and even less in the way of future prospects. Nothing to look forward to other than growing older and gradually sinking into a life of inactivity and acceptance of the inevitable.

Their thinking is refreshingly different, fuelled by enthusiasm; expectancy and anticipation. It's all about embracing life and living for the moment, unshackled by conformity and free from the fear of limitations that growing older once heralded.

## Consider your own attitude to being 60

So where do you stand (or comfortably sit) on the subject of your own age at the time of reaching sixty?

Have you accepted the challenge and decided that it is no

barrier to you having a fulfilling life, looking good, feeling fit and enjoying every moment of it? Free of hard-wired negative beliefs about age and its consequences?

Or have you taken the easier route and fully embraced sixty, as an opportunity to grow old? Forgetting about your appearance; not taking enough responsibility for your health; showing no interest in new challenges; forgetting about learning new skills and looking forward to your afternoon nap?

If you feel that you are slipping or have already fallen into this second group and are not sure what to do about it then now is the time to open your mind. There is most definitely a better way and it is waiting for you to take advantage of it.

The choice is yours and yours alone when it comes to deciding what you want from your life. We all have freedom of choice when it comes to our attitude to age and how we deal with it and there is little or no excuse to blame our environment or other convenient factors such as our finances; our partner or how we have lived our lives to date. Remember, it is sometimes hard, if not impossible, to change many of these factors, but it is possible to change ourselves. In particular our thoughts and attitudes can be changed if we really want to and have enough internal strength and resolve to do so.

It requires not only a positive and strong mental approach but also a plan for the changes you want to make. The changes you want and need may sometimes be difficult to specifically identify and can become blurred into a general desire simply to change. Establishing clear goals will help you enormously and give you direction and purpose which you may otherwise lack and which could scupper your best intentions.

## So, do you want to Make The Most Of *It*?

*It* is, of course, the rest of your life, however long it may last.

The most important thing is to get the most out of every day and enjoy each and every one of them. Having a personal commitment to living in the best way possible… being happy, healthy and fulfilled.

If you do, the rest of this book gives you ideas and a great starting point in deciding how to do so and how to treat reaching the age of sixty as a new beginning, or a new stage in your life, when so much is still possible and only your mind-set can stand in the way.

So where do you start? What changes should you be considering? What order should they be in? Have you got the will power to succeed?

Read On!

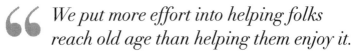 *We put more effort into helping folks reach old age than helping them enjoy it.*
Frank A Clark

- ◎ Challenge in your own mind the concept that sixty is an old age.
- ◎ Question the validity of your own belief system about age.
- ◎ Attitudes to age have changed dramatically and continue to do so.
- ◎ Have you personally got a positive attitude about growing older?
- ◎ Only you can change the way you think about age.
- ◎ Maximise and enjoy every day.
- ◎ Treat reaching sixty as a new beginning and a fresh and exciting phase of your life.

# 2.

## MAKING A PLAN FOR *IT*

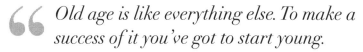 *Old age is like everything else. To make a success of it you've got to start young.*

Theodore Roosevelt

A great place to start is to use the age of sixty as the opportunity to take time out to evaluate where you are in your life. Take time to think about what you want to do with it from thereon in and how you are going to Make The Most Of *It*.

Consider how happy you feel and how satisfied you are with where you are at in your life. Do you feel fulfilled or are you frustrated with the way things are? Is the future looking good or is the outlook bleak?

If you have negative answers to these questions then you need to act now. Only *you* can make the changes.

Dare yourself to forget all the rules about age and consider setting your own personal agenda instead. If there are things you really want to do in this important phase of your life be prepared to push back all the boundaries you have established in your mind. You'll probably find that once you do, you'll discover and realise that others have already done so.

Of course, it is possible that you may already be quite

content with the way you are but equally you may be desperately unhappy, but either way, it is a good time to stop and give some serious consideration to the future if you really want to Make The Most Of *It*.

## Identify your current situation

The place to start is to look at the reality of your current situation in all areas of your life. Are you truly happy with what you are doing on a day to day basis; are all your relationships good; are you as fit and as healthy as you would like to be; do you look good for your age; have you got your finances under control; do you have regrets; is there something you always wanted to do that you have never got around to? What ambitions are still burning inside you and what is stopping you from doing these things?

These are just some of the important questions you need to ask yourself. It is a good idea to write each one down as it pops into your mind and make a list of all the areas in your life you want to reassess. Once you have made your list you can start thinking of what you consider your answers are. It may turn out to be a long list!

When you have given each of them enough consideration (don't take forever; time is marching on!) you can write down your thoughts next to each question. If you are really truthful to yourself this can be a brutal exercise as none of us likes to acknowledge our own shortcomings or weaknesses. It may be difficult, but how can you expect to make things better for yourself or achieve your unrealised ambitions unless you are honest enough to acknowledge what is currently wrong in your life?

Admitting that areas of our lives are not as good we would like, is the same as owning up to a personal failure, which is something none of us likes to admit. But if you want to make changes and lead that fulfilled life – if you want to Make The Most Of *It* – this is the only place to start. It is no good muddling on, expecting things to improve of their own accord or for someone else to make improvements for you, because it is very likely that it will never happen.

## Your wake-up call for change

This self-examination exercise is your wakeup call when you face the reality of your current existence in greater detail than ever before and with an analysis of exactly what is wrong in each specific area of your life.

It is so important because once you have considered the reality of where you currently are, you will be in a much better position to start planning for the future, as you will have a far clearer idea of the areas in your life that need to be improved. These thoughts and ideas will no longer be swirling around in your brain in an undefined and unidentified series of emotions and thoughts causing you unrest and anxiety. By this time you will have begun to have a greater understanding of what is stopping you from feeling fulfilled and achieving greater satisfaction and thus happiness from your life.

It may well be that you are not desperately unhappy with everything, or even anything, in your life but you do still have

21

those nagging doubts that all is not perfect. You may well feel that there must be more to it and you have, instead, settled for an easy life of mediocrity instead of stretching yourself to achieve even more from yourself.

As you are reading these words, those nagging thoughts may already be flitting through your mind, like a buzzing mosquito inside your head, really annoying you, because you know that, like that mosquito, you need to deal with them.

Identifying all the areas in your life which you would like to change or improve is a great way of starting to feel that you are taking charge of your life… the basis of a plan for the future is starting to develop. Taking control of your life and your future creates a great feeling of self-empowerment; a tangible feeling of liberation, creating hope, expectation and excitement. The sense of helplessness will start to diminish as you begin to feel positive once more.

## Setting your goals

Identifying these areas of concern is indeed the basis and first step for changes in your life. The next thing you need to do is to look at each of the areas you have identified and to consider all the possible opportunities you have to make changes to each of them to bring about the results that would be ideal for you.

This is how you are going to Make The Most Of *It*.

### Be realistic

Not an easy task and not a five-minute job to set your goals, as you may be thinking about some fairly radical changes, so one of your first considerations will be to fully understand the consequences of your proposed actions, both to yourself and others close to you.

For example, your desire to travel and see far off lands may not be as simple as giving up your job and leaving everybody behind to fend for themselves as you disappear into the sunset – as tempting as it may sometimes seem! Life is never quite that simple, particularly when you have already chalked up sixty years of it, because it is very possible that it is heavily intertwined with the lives of others.

So in setting your goals there will be some basic considerations that need to be taken into account, so a good place to start is to consider whether or not your goals are realistic as well as achievable.

Although we might think that there are no limits to our desires, in reality there are some which may prevent those desires being fulfilled. These limitations will come in all shapes and forms, such as financial; physical and time restraints.

Thus, if you dream of buying a luxury home in a glamorous resort, it is going to be very tricky to achieve that ambition if you do not have the money. It may still be possible if you win the lottery or become an internet millionaire but the reality of the situation is, that it is unlikely to happen, so if your goal is to own one of these homes you may well end up being very disappointed. Not a great start to enjoying the rest of your life.

Equally, if as you turn sixty you decide that you want to win the London marathon, there is an extremely good chance that this ambition will also fail because it was totally unrealistic in the first instance. Age should not be a barrier but it can begin to impose some limitations, particularly when it comes to physical prowess.

### Be mindful of how long it will take

Time is also an issue when setting your goals for change and for the future. If you want to learn a new skill that is going to take ten years to learn fully, do you really want to give up so much of your time to achieving it? If the answer is yes, then you may well be able to learn that skill but if not, the goal will be unachievable and you will end up being frustrated and unhappy. Obviously, not the most desirable of outcomes from a goal that was supposed to make you feel more fulfilled.

So it is really important to set your goals with all these thoughts in mind if you want to avoid disappointment. It is simply being realistic. This does not automatically mean that you need to be un-ambitious in the changes you set for yourself. Not at all, because if you really want to do something and you feel that it is within your capabilities, then you must go for it. After all the idea is to Make The Most Of It.

It's just very important to make sure that your goals are clear and that you believe they are achievable before you commit yourself to them.

### Be specific

One more important point to consider before setting your goals is that you need to make sure that you are specific when you do so. It is very easy to be quite vague at the outset which means that ultimately you are never quite sure whether or not you have achieved the goal.

For example, if your goal is 'to get fitter' how do you know if you have achieved this unless you can somehow measure it? Better to set a goal that is much more clearly defined. For example if your goal is to be able to swim fifty lengths of the swimming pool without stopping, instead of the two of which you are currently capable, then you have set a very clear and measurable goal. Not only can you measure what you have achieved you can be sure that you have got fitter in doing so.

Similarly, if your goal is to be 'happier in the future', you need to clarify how can you measure this because an emotion like happiness is subjective and can vary so much from day to day. Better to have set out to make a change in your life that is likely to result in greater happiness for you, for example finding a new relationship or finding work or a pastime that you really enjoy. You will be in a position to know for certain when you have achieved your goal and in doing so you should experience greater happiness in your life as a result.

So the task of setting your goals is not to be rushed and you need to follow these simple rules. Make them:

◎ Realistic
◎ Achievable in an acceptable time frame
◎ Specific

Finally you must make goals that, once achieved, will bring you a sense of achievement, satisfaction and fulfilment and in doing so ensure that you Make The Most Of *It*.

Remember also that it is always better to have tried and failed than never to have tried at all. Just the very fact that you are trying will bring you greater satisfaction as well as giving enjoyment along the way.

## Managing your plan

Having identified the key areas in your life that you want to improve, or in which to do something different, you are well on your way to creating your own life-changing plan. Your plan will enable you to clearly establish the things in your life that you feel are currently not as good as you want them to be, and what you believe is wrong. Your plan will have also identified what changes you want to make and the goals you have set for yourself.

You have arrived at the point where you are really starting to take control of your future and ensuring that from sixty onwards you are going to be doing what you want to do rather than drifting through the rest of your life.

At this point it is important to be aware, however, that like all good plans, they are only as good as the commitment and determination of the person who is to implement them… which, of course, is you!

### *Have you got the willpower?*

Unless you have the will to carry out what you have planned then the goals will never be achieved. They will simply be good intentions that never materialised into reality. Broken dreams of achieving a more meaningful existence, leaving you feeling even more frustrated than before as your years slip by.

So once you have identified your clear and important goals, the goals that you want to achieve once you are sixty, you must then ask yourself how likely you are to be successful. On a scale of one to ten, score your determination to achieve each of your goals. Make a list of all of you goals and enter next to each one your score based on your determination to succeed.

If you are ultimately to be successful in achieving each desired goal, you should have scored your level of willpower to do so, to be at least nine out of ten in each case. If in respect of any individual goal you have scored less than nine, you need to ask yourself; 'Why?'

Is it because the goal you have set is, in fact, more of a fanciful wish on your part?

Or is it that you feel that it might just be too much like hard work to achieve the goal and you doubt your own resolve to see it through?

These are important questions to ask yourself and once you have, you will then need to decide whether you can improve on your will to succeed, or if not, whether you should alter or abandon the goal.

One thing is certain: there is no point in planning to do things to make the most of your life if you do not have the will to succeed, because failure is very likely to make you feel deeply disappointed and even more unfulfilled than you were before.

Once you have determined that you do have the necessary level of will power to turn those goals into reality you are now ready to get on with it and start making the changes that will bring you greater happiness and that tremendous feeling of fulfilment.

Before we look at how to progress with your plan we need to spend time just considering in more detail some of those key areas of your life that are possibly going to be those, in which you want to make changes.

 *The whole business about marshalling one's energies becomes more and more important as one grows old.*

Hume Cronyn

---

**MEMORY JOGGERS**

---

◎ Carry out an evaluation of the important components of your life.

◎ Be honest with yourself in considering what is stopping you from being happy and feeling fulfilled.

◎ Set your own personal agenda for changes you want to make.

◎ Always try to be realistic about what you plan to do.

◎ The changes you make need to be planned to have a positive impact on your life.

◎ You need determination to achieve your goals.

# 3.

## HEALTH, FITNESS AND MENTAL WELL-BEING

> *You can't help getting older, but you don't have to get old.*
>
> George Burns

One thing about life, that you are more than likely to have realised by now, is that without good health, enjoyable living can become difficult and many things cannot be achieved. It matters little how much money you have, or what desirable goals you want to set yourself, if your health prevents you from enjoying these things.

It is therefore good news that in recent years we have witnessed continuing improving statistics concerning life expectancy in many countries. In the United Kingdom in 2012 the average life expectancy was eighty-one, compared to seventy-eight in the year 2000. In the USA statistics were very similar, with life expectancy being seventy-nine in 2012 as opposed to seventy-seven in 2000. Similar statistics prevail in most western European countries and throughout the world in modernised nations with advanced health care and good living conditions such as Australia; New Zealand; Canada and Singapore.

Importantly, as well, The World Health Organisation (WHO) statistics from 2012 also reveal that once you successfully reach the age of sixty in both the UK and the USA you can, on average, expect to live another twenty-three years (for a male twenty-two and a female twenty-five years). On a global basis it is estimated that everyone who reaches sixty has, on average, another twenty years to live.

These are encouraging statistics that prove to each of us that there is plenty of life to be lived once we reach sixty and that life expectancy continues to improve as time progresses.

However, these figures are only averages so the key question is, on which side of the average do you want to fall? This is where your own well-being becomes totally relevant because these statistics count for nothing if your own body and mind are in poor shape.

Do you want to beat that average and give yourself even more time to achieve your goals or will your previous lifestyle let you down and as a consequence prevent you from reaching even the average life expectancy?

## How healthy are you?

You will have a fair idea for yourself what condition you are in and, if you have failed to adequately look after your health as you approach sixty, then this may be one of the key areas that you are now looking to change for the better. After all, we all want to live as long as possible as well as Making The Most Of It.

There are numerous factors to consider when we assess our own well-being and again it is necessary for us to be honest with ourselves about the short comings in our lifestyles that have resulted in our current condition.

For example you may be conscious that you are overweight and wanting to trim down a bit to feel healthier and fitter as well as looking slimmer.

Or you may have lived with habits which have been identified as being bad for your health such as smoking; excessive indulgence in alcohol or drugs abuse.

You may not have taken care of your diet in the way the health professionals advise us and have been eating too much junk food and not enough of the recommended fruit and vegetables.

You may have avoided regular health check-ups and now feel concerned about the state of your blood pressure or cholesterol levels. Some of us prefer not to know if something is wrong and ignore the warning signs of a problem, hoping that it will go away. Unfortunately, it rarely does.

If you have not exercised regularly you will probably be aware of how unfit you are and how this is now limiting your ability to be as active as you would wish. At the same time you may have taken little interest in your own physical appearance and grooming so apart from not feeling that healthy you don't look particularly good either.

Your mental health may have suffered as a result of stressful living caused by your work or your domestic situation or even your finances. This can take a huge toll on our ability to enjoy our lives and to feel positive about the future.

You may be able to identify with one or more of these or

other similar issues and have been meaning to do something about it for some time but have never quite got around to it. Sometimes it is easier to put off until tomorrow those things that we find unpleasant or difficult and the result is that they continue to get put off and never get done. Procrastination is rarely the wisest route to follow when it comes to looking after your health.

If you can identify with any of these thoughts and are feeling a little guilty about your own procrastination then reaching sixty is as good a place as any to really take stock of your physical and mental state.

If you are going to pursue an active and interesting life from this point on then you need to stop thinking about it and actually start doing it. It will be no easier tomorrow if you wait another day and, in fact, once you have started making changes you are going to feel a whole lot better, both physically and mentally.

One thing is fairly certain is that if you have not taken care of yourself to date then eventually you are likely to be affected with health problems which will seriously affect your ability to make the most of it. Remember on average you are likely to live at least another twenty-three years after you turn sixty. That's an awful long time and a great opportunity for you to ensure that you really do Make The Most Of *It!*

### Identifying how you need to improve your health

You will probably already know for yourself the areas affecting your health and it is in these that you should seriously be thinking about making changes and focussing your plan.

## Physical fitness

If you have never got around to exercising regularly then you probably feel unfit and may be experiencing other possible side effects such as being overweight and not being as mobile as you would wish. You probably feel your bones creaking as you get out of bed every morning!

Your plan will probably identify your lack of fitness and getting fitter will be one of your key goals. In doing so you will have identified what is currently unsatisfactory and what needs to improve. If you want to change you will then need to choose how you can start to exercise and how best to do that. In doing so, there will be key factors to consider, the achievement of which will be vital if you are to be successful.

Firstly, you will need to find a form of exercise which you will enjoy; which is affordable and which is readily available to you. It is no good choosing something, in which it will be difficult for you to participate.

For example, if you wanted to exercise by swimming but there is no pool conveniently located then you are defeated before you start. Or if you wanted to join the local gym but could not afford the membership fees then you will have to strike that one off your list.

So find something that is affordable to you; which is convenient; which interests you and will help you to get fitter. Once you start really looking with serious intent you will be surprised at the number and variety of opportunities available to you.

Even if you have kidded yourself into believing that there

is nothing, think again! The cheapest and easiest way to start exercising is to walk. Wherever you live, if you are mobile, you can go out for a walk, so there is no excuse to do nothing.

So if getting fitter by exercising regularly is a goal for you within your Making The Most Of *It* plan, you can now get on and decide how you are going to do it. Just remember that you need to set yourself a measurable goal over your decided time frame so that you can be sure that you achieve a definite improvement in your fitness level.

The goal will depend on your favoured method of exercise and is for you to decide. You may also want to establish different stages to achieve so that it becomes a progressive goal over a period of time.

For example, if walking is your preferred way of exercising your goal may initially be to walk one mile, three times a week and you want to be able to achieve that regularly for a month. That's your first goal identified.

Once you have achieved that you may want to set a new goal of walking two miles each time or you may also want to increase the number of times you walk each week.

This progressive setting of exercise goals will enable you to steadily build up to an improved level of fitness and can be gauged to suit your lifestyle and capabilities. The great thing is that all the time you are gradually getting fitter and feeling the benefits of doing so.

There is no need to feel downhearted if sometimes you don't quite manage to achieve the goal you have set yourself because circumstances can change and external events can intervene. Simply adjust your plans and carry on as soon as you are able to do so. Plans should always be realistic but sometimes you may find that your goals will need to be flexible as well.

Working progressively to achieve your fitness goals can be applied to whatever form of exercise you choose and there is no reason for you not to pursue more than one type of exercise at a time. The choice is yours and as long as you exercise within your capabilities you can go on gradually getting fitter and a whole lot healthier.

You may even find that exercising creates new friendships for you and opens other areas of interest because there are plenty of other people out there who will be doing similar things. If you have a partner they may also want to participate in the exercise which is always a good thing because it helps to have someone urging you on when the going sometimes gets tough!

If you have doubts about the validity of exercise as a good way of improving your health you need look no further than the UK's National Health Service (NHS) website.

The NHS refers to exercise as 'The miracle cure we've all been waiting for'.

If you doubt the validity of that statement then you should also be aware that they support it by suggesting that regular exercise can reduce your risk of major illness, such as heart disease, stroke, diabetes and cancer by up to 50% and lower your risk of an early death by up to 30%.

All this from something which can be free, easy and have an immediate effect!

### *Dealing with addiction*

Of course, if your health has suffered from an addiction to smoking, alcohol or drugs then lack of exercise will not be the only problem that you face. Addiction can arise because we have something missing in our lives and all our needs are not being met. Unfortunately, addiction can be very destructive and can prevent us from leading really satisfied lives.

This addiction may be something that you want to get to grips with at this important time in your life and there is definitely still time in your life to make a change and benefit as a result.

There are many depressing statistics available to support the ill effects of addiction to harmful substances and there can be no doubting their validity, but even so these habits can be hard to kick. It is easy to be full of good intentions when it comes to dealing with an addiction but quite often these good intentions are rather like New Year's resolutions: you start off with enthusiasm but soon fall by the wayside as day to day life takes over again.

There exists, however, in most modern societies, help which is available to support those who wish to overcome their addiction. Starting with your local doctor information can be obtained indicating where and how help is available and this is a good starting point. Overcoming any addictive habit can be very difficult and this is why professional help and support are vital if you are to be successful. There are trained professionals who will understand your problem and be able to give you real and practical help which will reinforce your own determination to make a change for the good.

So once again your plan starts by identifying what it is you want to change and why you need to do so. You need to be totally honest with yourself and be clear with your goal because if you are not then it is only you who will suffer the consequences of failure and the associated disappointment.

You then need to look at all the opportunities that are available to you to start making a change and make a list of all your options. Apart from your doctor, the internet offers an amazing resource which will provide you with information concerning where you can obtain practical help and support close to where you live.

Be careful only to seek help from properly qualified sources and avoid trying to deal with your habit by using self-help suggestions you may read about. Dealing with addiction is difficult if you have no support and encouragement. Now is the time to seek the right professional help and this is a good initial starting point as part of your goal to overcome your habit and improve your health.

Taking small but important steps will make it easier to be successful than just trying to achieve a big goal from the outset. Once you have made up your mind that you want to deal with your addiction, finding a source of help and support is a really important first step. Learning something new involves taking things slowly like a child learning to walk. You will find that one small step at a time is easier than trying to run straight away.

From there you can move on, with the proper help and support, to deal with the issue in a planned and timely manner.

It may be a long journey but, after all, you have plenty of time left to enjoy your life and it will be so much better to do so free of your addiction.

The potential rewards from dealing with your addiction can be numerous. These can include improved physical health; greater self-respect and mental well-being; financial savings; and more time. All of these will greatly contribute to you Making The Most Of *It*.

### *Establishing a healthy diet*

Most of us will be aware that our eating habits can have a major effect on our health and well-being. We are constantly being told that fast foods contain all the things we should not be eating and we should be ensuring that we do eat plenty of fruit and vegetables and non-processed foods. Even though we know these things, many of us still choose to ignore the warnings and advice. This is another example of how we often believe that 'it will never happen to me'.

As you read this you may be aware that your own eating and drinking habits have been unsatisfactory and as a result there have been some unhealthy consequences for you. You may be overweight; suffer from high cholesterol or blood pressure or just generally feel not too healthy. Any of these issues can not only make you feel physically out of shape but can also make you feel mentally pretty miserable too.

If you are feeling down you are more prone to eat more to try and cheer yourself up so it can become a vicious circle. Sugar intake in particular can give you a quick fix but this feeling soon disappears only to be replaced with a craving for more. Feeling this way is also likely to affect your self-motivation so when it comes to making an effort to enjoy yourself you may find it difficult to summon up enough energy and enthusiasm.

Establishing a healthy diet, to both undo some of the damage you have already done and to feel better in the future, may be a significant area of change for you. It may have been niggling away in your mind but you have never quite got around to getting to grips with it. If you are to maximise your life you will need to make sure that you give yourself every advantage and a good diet and eating habits could be of enormous help.

### So what difference can diet make?

Eating healthy foods can encourage weight loss; promote energy levels; improve physical appearance and well-being while avoiding the problems created by obesity. With so many proven benefits it is amazing how often good eating habits are ignored as the craze for junk and unhealthy foods prevails.

Now consider this. An unhealthy diet can lead to a greater risk of contracting a chronic disorder such as heart disease; diabetes; cancer and other serious conditions. Medical research has proven that the risk of contracting these conditions can significantly be reduced by eating less salt, sugar and saturated fats and by eating more fruit, vegetables, nuts and grains.

Most people are already very aware of these facts but have chosen to ignore them in the past often because of a lack of self-discipline. Often low income is blamed yet it is no more expensive to eat healthy foods than it is to consume a bad diet. In fact, the opposite may apply and you may find that buying and preparing fresh foods yourself is cheaper than buying processed foods and takeaways. What you put in your mouth and eat is your decision but really it is just as easy, and will cost no more, to eat what is good for you.

If you have been one of those who have lacked some self-discipline in your eating habits and this has resulted in you being overweight you may now want to lose weight and enjoy the benefits of doing so. This may well be one of your major goals in Making The Most Of *It*.

There are numerous ways to approach dieting and establish healthier eating and there are many organisations helping people to do so. Whatever your chosen method, and there are many, none of them will work unless you commit yourself to achieving your goal and have the willpower to see it through.

### Weight loss made manageable

A good and simple way to approach weight loss is to target gradual loss within a planned timescale. For example, you may target yourself to losing a kilo, or two pounds, every calendar month and continue to do so until you reach your desired weight. This is far more manageable and easier to monitor than setting yourself an enormous and unrealistic target over an extended time period.

You may have heard people talk about losing weight and planning to lose a large amount of weight in a short time frame. Other than starving yourself, which is not very desirable, this is not an easy task. Losing weight gradually is healthier for you and gives your body and mind time to gradually adjust to a new and healthier way of eating.

You need to retrain yourself so that eating less, and consuming more healthy foods, just becomes a natural part of your daily lifestyle. After a while you will find that you no longer crave for the unhealthy food that formed your diet previously.

### *Get support to help you*

It is also important to have support along the way using something like a weight loss club which not only will monitor your progress but also offer practical support and advice. Group sessions also promote peer pressure which may be of benefit when your resistance levels drop and you start reaching for the biscuit jar!

If you are living with other people it will obviously make changing your eating habits much easier if they are supportive and encourage you. Problems can arise however when their own eating habits are not as good as yours because they may try to discourage you. They may become jealous of your success in losing weight when they are unable or unwilling to do so themselves. They may want to see you fail so they can turn to you and say 'I told you so'. In these circumstances it will be vital to have outside help which is supportive and gives you encouragement.

Eating healthier; losing weight and generally improving your health are all areas of self-improvement, in which many people feel the need to engage during their lives and it is better to do so before suffering the consequences associated with a poor diet. So why wait any longer?

To ensure that you can maximise your life and future enjoyment from sixty onwards it may well be the right time for you to put this change on your priority list. Only you will know.

## Stress and anxiety

If you feel that your life is being detrimentally affected by something that causes you stress or anxiety then your life plan gives you the ideal opportunity to try and do something about it.

Many people live with stress and yet seek to do little about it and as a consequence suffer both physically and mentally.

Stress can cause numerous physical symptoms such as sleeplessness, headaches, restlessness, loss of appetite, weight loss, over-eating and weight gain, skin conditions and poor concentration. These in turn can add to your level of stress and make you feel even worse.

Mentally it can bring on memory loss, mood swings and preoccupation. Instead of feeling ready to greet everyday with enthusiasm you will probably feel more inclined to crawl back under the bed covers and give the day a miss.

The physical and mental effects of stress can have a major influence on many different aspects of your life and can seriously affect relationships, work and careers, and restrict participation in numerous activities, to leave the sufferer with little expectation of a happy and fulfilling future. Your enthusiasm for life will be dulled as you are preoccupied with your feelings. There seems to be no escape from your feelings because it is all you can think and talk about.

This in turn can cause further problems as some people will seek to avoid you because they do not want to hear about your problems.

### Do you have stress in your life?

If you are aware of stress in your life, and can recognise some of these symptoms in yourself, then as you approach sixty you need to clearly establish an action plan to help you deal with this serious issue. You really cannot afford to let stress and anxiety get in the way as you set out to maximise the rest of your life. If you fail to deal with it you are unlikely to be able to commit yourself to even drawing up your life plan, let alone setting out to accomplish your goals.

In dealing with stress there are practical steps that can be taken to help in the short term. These may involve exercise; medication; leisure activities and so on. They will undoubtedly help and bring some temporary respite from feeling stressed. However, in the long-term the only way to deal with it is to identify what is causing the problem and, once you have done so, seek to rectify it. This can often be difficult to do by yourself and the assistance of a professional may offer the best solution. This may be found by using a suitably qualified counsellor or psychotherapist who will help you to identify the causes of stress in your life and guide you to finding ways of dealing with it.

You may be wary of sharing your thoughts and feelings with someone you do not know but discussing these with a qualified therapist in a safe environment can be very helpful. They will be impartial and confidential and offer a safer approach than discussing your feelings with either relatives or a friend, who may be tempted to give you opinions and advice which may be unhelpful.

It is certain that living with stress and anxiety over a prolonged period of time will take its toll on any individual. While there may not be a quick and simple approach to deal with it, what is important is to understand that doing nothing is very unlikely to make the stress go away. You may take an aspirin to temporarily make your headache go away but unless you find out what is causing the headache in the first instance, it is likely to reoccur. The same applies to stress – you may find that you can gain temporary relief but the stress will return if the true cause is not addressed.

If stress and anxiety have affected you and you want to enjoy the rest of your life free of these burdens, then seeking help is a priority for you and the sooner you take action the sooner you will start to feel better. If not, your ability to Make The Most Of *It* will be seriously diminished.

 *Life expectancy would grow by leaps and bounds if green vegetables smelled as good as bacon.*

Doug Larson

- ◎ Good mental and physical health will help you get the best out of your life.
- ◎ Have you put off getting sorted any health problems you have?
- ◎ Make exercise easier by doing something you enjoy.
- ◎ Work progressively to improve your fitness.
- ◎ Dealing with addiction needs professional help.
- ◎ Have a good and honest look at your eating and drinking habits.
- ◎ Losing weight is easier in small amounts rather than attempting drastic losses.
- ◎ To deal with stress on a permanent basis you need to identify and deal with the root cause.

# 4.

## RELATIONSHIPS...
## WHAT'S THE POINT OF THEM?

> *When you stop expecting people to be perfect, you can like them for who they are.*
>
> Donald Miller

We have all heard the expression that 'No man (or woman) is an island' (John Donne), which simply means that it is extremely difficult to live our lives in isolation from other human beings. Some have tried a hermit style of living but, apart from all our other needs, the very perpetuity of the human race depends upon relationships.

Of course, the relationships we experience throughout our lifetimes extend far wider than just our sexual relationships with a chosen partner.

Even before we are born we have the security and nurturing which our mother provides and, once born, the family unit will normally give us a number of close and long lasting relationships. The family bond is, for many, the strongest form of relationship that they will experience during their lifetime. Even if there is some falling out along the way, the fact that you have that blood relationship means that the bond will always exist.

As we grow, passing through childhood and then adolescence, our relationship circle gradually extends to encompass friends, neighbours, teachers and team mates. Once we reach our teens we also start to experience relationships based on physical attraction as we begin to explore the need to have a partner, falling in love and sexual attraction.

New relationships continue to develop throughout our lives as we move from education to work, where there are completely new and exciting opportunities to meet new people outside our existing relationship circle.

At some time we may marry or live with a partner, possibly changing priorities within our relationships as that partner becomes the most important person in your life. At the same time an abundance of new relationships may be formed as we become involved in our new partners' existing relationships with their family and friends. Priorities are likely to change again if children come along as a result of that partnership.

Relationships rarely stand still in our lives and are likely to continually change and evolve as we progress through life and our circumstances change.

## Relationships are beneficial to us
Through all of these relationships we can gain enormous benefits such as companionship, love, procreation, security, friendship, self-esteem and a feeling of well-being. They are of great benefit to us and help maintain our mental well-being.

The value of relationships should not be underestimated at any time in our lives and this continues to hold true as we get older.

However, as we do grow older our needs can change in many ways and this can affect what we want or expect from a relationship even though the other person may not feel the same way. Relationships can therefore change or cease all together as time progresses. You may have already experienced this, particularly in the case of friendships formed at various times in your life which have slowly faded away as you progress through life and circumstances change for both of you.

If you cast your mind back you will probably be able to record numerous relationships that temporarily existed throughout your life but for one reason or another exist now only as a memory. Possibly as a pleasant memory, but for others, possibly not!

## Identify what you want from your relationships

So as we reach the age of sixty, what relationships do we have and what do feel that we really want or need from those relationships?

There can be little doubt that, once we stop and think about it, having strong personal relationships as we grow older is probably the key factor in being able to have and enjoy a happy later life. This goal should be a priority in Making The Most Of It.

Uppermost in our minds may be that we want to avoid being lonely as we grow older and have no-one to love or be loved by. Loneliness can be a dreadful problem for many as they grow older particularly with so many marriages and partnerships ending in failure, even after many years of being together.

In recent years divorce rates for the over-sixties have risen even though divorce rates, generally, have fallen.

There appears to be a number of reasons why we are now seeing more couples in their sixties separating. Obviously with people increasingly living longer, there are more people of that age, which in itself is likely to increase the numbers divorcing. However, attitudes to divorce have changed significantly and there is no longer any stigma attached to it as used to be the case. There is also a much larger percentage of women working nowadays, who have consequently become more financially independent and are likely to have built up their own pension pot. Separating is a lot easier if you know that it will not result in financial hardship.

We should also remember that we can still look forward to living for some time after we reach sixty and if you feel unhappy in your current relationship it is not too late to do something about it. Divorce may be considered the last resort in making a change but nevertheless, with divorce laws being much easier in current times, it is an option which some elect.

If we are fortunate enough to feel that we are still cared for and have good relationships within our family, as well as with close friends and others we know, then this knowledge gives us a tremendous sense of security which can bring us peace of mind. We can feel positive and reassured about our future lives because of those relationships and the various types of support they give us.

Basically, these relationships can give us a real sense of worth and well-being and if you are going to Make The Most Of It, what better way to enjoy it than to share your time with people with whom you have a good relationship? After all, if, as you reach sixty, you feel lonely, isolated and uncared for, you probably will be totally unmotivated when it comes to getting on and having a great time in life. Who are you going to share all this pleasure with?

## Thinking about your own relationships

So where do you start when thinking about your own relationships and what they are providing for you? Probably a good place to start is to ask yourself the following simple question:

'Which relationships are important to me and am I getting the most out of them?'

The first task is to identify the existing relationships you already have and categorise them by way of priority and importance to you. This can be done by creating a relationship circle which has three bands to it and looks like this:

*The Relationship Circle*

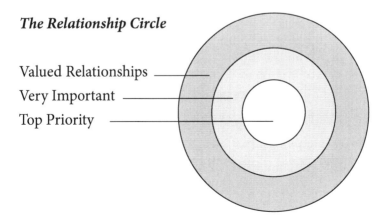

Valued Relationships
Very Important
Top Priority

At the very centre of your Relationship Circle are your Top Priority Relationships. These are the people that are most important to you and are always likely to be so. They may include your partner; children; grand-children and the very closest of friends. It is up to you to decide who is included but these should be relationships which are really important to you and are always likely to be so even as time progresses and circumstances change.

In the second band of your Relationship Circle you should enter the names of those people that are Important Relationships to you. These are likely to be people that you get on well with and with whom you enjoy contact, but are not as close as those in your priority circle.

Finally, in the outer band of your Relationship Circle, enter the names of those people, with whom you have a relationship and, while being Valued Relationships, they are not as close as the two previous categories.

This entire exercise, in itself, should prove to be seriously thought-provoking for you. At the age of sixty, you will be identifying the key relationships that you currently have and possibly at the same time it may be illustrating to you that your circle of relationships is either far greater or smaller than you had realised.

Of course, even though you have identified the importance of each relationship to you, it does not necessarily follow that each relationship is as good as it might be. A relationship may be an important one for you simply because you all have to live under the same roof but it does not necessarily follow that all is right within it. The key to contentment in all relationships is whether or not both parties are satisfied with what they are getting out it. If there is a perceived imbalance in the benefits, that one or the other parties to the relationship is getting out of it, then there is likely to be discontentment.

You may already be aware of this within some of your relationships.

## How happy are your relationships?

Starting with the people in your priority list of relationships take each one in turn and consider how happy you are with that relationship. At this time there is no point in trying to consider what the other person may feel about the relationship because the only thing that matters at this stage is how you feel.

On a scale of zero to ten, score how happy you are with each of your priority relationships, with zero being utterly unhappy, and ten being ecstatic. We can call this The Happiness Scale.

This may take some time and some serious consideration, particularly as each person will mean something different to you and will make you happy, or be very important to you, in different ways.

For example, if you have a partner and you are considering how you feel about them, the important aspects of the relationship you have with them will be substantially different to those you would be considering if you were thinking about a grand-child. Both relationships would be extremely important to you and would therefore probably fall into your priority category but what you expected to get out of them would be largely different.

We all know that few people are perfect (except ourselves!) and thus to score a perfect ten for a priority relationship may not always be honest or possible but if you can score those relationships as high as eight out of ten then you have a pretty sound and rewarding relationship.

Once you have scored a relationship you then need to identify and list the areas, which you see as negative and preventing you from feeling completely happy about the relationship. What needs to change for you to be able to score that relationship as ten out of ten? This exercise will help you to understand *specifically* what would need to be different, for you to feel completely happy in your relationship with that person.

Once you have considered all of your relationships in this way you are in a better position to be able to understand how much they contribute to your enjoyment and satisfaction of life.

Start with your list of priority relationships. If you have some which have scored badly, using the Happiness scale, you are unlikely to be content and happy in life and probably not in a good place to Make The Most Of *It*. Too many things are wrong and unsatisfactory within your important relationships to make possible your peace of mind and contentment. If a number of your key relationships are not as you would like them, your contentment level is unlikely to be as strong as it could be.

## Improving your relationships

So what can *you* do about those relationships which are not as good as they should be? If you can improve them, would it make your life more enjoyable and happy? The answer is likely to be a resounding 'Yes!'

The first place to start trying to improve a relationship is to identify, and then try and change, the issues that are causing the problems between you. This may not be simple to do, but you need to consider if it is worth making the effort to put right what is wrong, for the benefit of that relationship. You may need to talk to the other person about what is making you unhappy to help find a solution or it might be simply that you have to make more effort yourself, such as communicating with them more frequently. If you fail to make the effort to share your life with others it should not be a surprise if they fail to share their life with you.

Sometimes we can become stubborn in relationships because we feel that the other person is not making as much effort as we are to improve the situation between us. We can feel that we are putting more into it than they are and probably getting less out of it. This is usually what happens when you have children as you seem to be the one who is making all the effort. However, with a child you are likely to tolerate this situation because you know that it will gradually change as they grow up. There is no guarantee however, that this will be the case!

In other cases you have to decide if this is a relationship you want to maintain and if you do, you may have to swallow your pride, put aside your stubbornness, and make even more effort yourself. Just remember that it is always easier to change yourself than to change somebody else, but at the same time you need to find a way to explain to the other person how you feel. Naturally, it will be much better if you can do this without arguing or being overly critical. Try and find more a more open and mature approach to communicate your feelings which is less likely to cause you to fall out even more!

By working through all of your priority relationships in this way, and taking each one in turn and assessing just how good it is, you will be able to decide on the courses of action you need to pursue. You will be taking control and making changes for your own happiness and enjoyment, which is likely to be a much healthier situation for yourself.

Gradually the same exercise can be applied to all the relationships you have and you can make decisions about each one as to whether or not they are good for you the way they are. From those decisions you can decide how to improve or enhance each one or maybe drop it all together. Your decision should be based on how much each relationship brings positive benefits to your life and future.

This is obviously not a quick exercise, nor is it likely to be a quick fix for making you happy, as relationships can be notoriously difficult to change if they have not been good for a while. Repairing or improving a relationship may take a considerable amount of time and effort and even then you may not be successful. For others, however, it may be as simple as picking up the 'phone to speak to somebody or sending them an email. You may be pleasantly surprised with the result.

## Why it's worth it

Good relationships offering love, companionship and friendship, or even just some of these benefits, can give each of us a tremendous feeling of contentment and well-being so they are well worth the effort. As with most things in life you frequently get out of something just as much as you are prepared to put in. So if you believe you are missing these things in your life you will need to make the effort to give just as much as you would like to receive. It will benefit no-one if a relationship is suffering just because you feel that the other party should be the one to make the first move.

Just remember that being alone and uncared for as we grow older is not a happy situation for any of us. Nor is it much joy trying to have fun and do exciting things when we have no-one, with whom to share it.

Ask yourself once more the question about the point of relationships and by now you will probably be even more aware just how important they are to you.

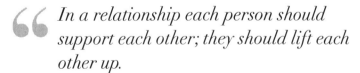 *In a relationship each person should support each other; they should lift each other up.*

Taylor Swift

- It is good for us to have sound relationships in our lives.
- Good relationships bring enormous benefits to us.
- Identify what you are looking for from your relationships at sixty.
- Loneliness is depressing.
- Sharing the fun in your life makes it even better.
- Examine the quality of your existing relationships.
- Relationships can be improved by changing the things which are causing problems.
- Get your relationships in shape and enjoy them!

# 5.

## MAKING NEW FRIENDS

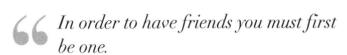 *In order to have friends you must first be one.*

Elbert Hubbard

After you have given due consideration to all of the existing relationships in your life and decided how you can improve them and, as a result, find them more rewarding, you will have taken a huge step in enhancing this extremely important aspect of your life.

You will have thought about ways to increase your happiness and sense of well-being by having improved relationships with others. Even in the non-intimate friendships you have, such as a friend with whom you share a hobby or meet only once in a while for a chat, the knowledge that they are pleased to spend time in your company is both comforting and rewarding.

For some of us, however, the exercise of examining our existing relationships can illustrate something, of which we are probably already aware, but have not been keen to acknowledge. That is, that we do not have enough relationships and good friends in our lives and as a consequence we can sometimes experience degrees of loneliness and feelings of isolation. This can not only be depressing, but if we feel uncared for, can also be damaging to our self-esteem and confidence. Few of us want to feel lonely in this way, particularly as we get older.

You would expect that after so many years of living your life you would have numerous good friends and close relationships (as well as a few not so good ones!) providing you with more than an adequate supply of love and friendship. Unfortunately, this is not always the case and a number of factors in modern living have contributed to this.

The family unit once provided a constancy of relationships even though they may not always have been happy ones. The modern family unit is not as stable as it once was with the separation and divorce of partners a commonplace event. This has resulted in many people becoming single once again at a time in their life when they did not expect it, as well as sometimes causing major fall-outs within the family and divided loyalties. It can also lead to a loss of friendships as a result of taking sides. It seems that the family unit is no longer guaranteed to give you the permanency in your relationships which it might have done in years gone by.

In addition, lifestyles have become more mobile, with people leaving their childhood homes to go off to study or work, not only in their own country but increasingly in foreign lands. Thus, families become distant and remote with communication no longer on a face–to–face basis but instead via a digital link. It is extremely difficult to give a loved one a hug via the internet.

Not only can this make relationships within your family more difficult and less personal, in can also result in the loss of contact with other good friends and acquaintances. The lifestyle of the modern world influenced by ease of mobility; the breakdown of the family unit and the use of remote communication does not readily lend itself to close relationships. No wonder that many people find themselves with a shortage of close family and friends, with whom to physically share life, just as they reach that stage when such relationships are hugely important for happiness and contentment.

So what can be done about it if you find yourself in this situation?

The good news is that there is plenty that you can do!

Once again it is important to think through what it is you want to improve and then organise yourself to create your plan to achieve it. As always, in making the most of the rest of your life, you need to think about opportunities for new relationships properly so that you achieve the desired result and not end up disappointed or disillusioned as well as wasting valuable time. This will only make you feel worse, rather than better, so good preparation is the key.

Your starting point is to consider the type of new relationship you need. Broadly speaking there are two categories: the intimate relationship of a new partner; or the friendship relationship in which you can spend time with another person.

## Seeking a new partner

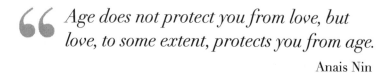 *Age does not protect you from love, but love, to some extent, protects you from age.*

Anais Nin

If, at the age of sixty, you are unattached and seeking a new partner, you may find the thought of finding and meeting someone new extremely daunting. This is likely to be the case if previously you have been in a long-term relationship which has ended leaving you feeling lonely and possibly disillusioned about love. Alternatively you may have possibly lost your partner due to bereavement and the thought of seeking a new relationship provokes conflicting emotions for you. In either case the thought of dating again may scare you silly!

Your mind may well be full of negative thoughts about yourself, particularly about your body image and your economic circumstances. You may also find it difficult to contemplate having an intimate relationship with someone new.

Those feelings are perfectly understandable and can be very difficult emotions to handle. You may also be concerned about what other people may think, for example your children, if you have any. However, you need to be bold and strong and try and set aside those feelings if they are holding you back from doing something that could be beneficial to you. You are entitled to make your own decisions about your future without seeking the approval of others.

Remember what they say about a faint heart when it comes

to romance. After all you will achieve nothing, if you do nothing, and if it goes well it could bring about a monumental change for the better in your life. You may feel your heart starting to beat faster just thinking about it!

Also you need to remember that being unattached and a free agent you can meet as many different people as you like and you can always say no. Eventually, however, there is always the chance that you may just meet the person who is perfect for you. It is always worth remembering that the person you meet will be there for the same reason as you; they also want to meet someone new, so you are sharing a common goal. This makes a positive outcome a far greater possibility.

### Internet dating

A perfect place to start, if you are looking for that new partner and romance, is the internet. This is without doubt the fastest growing and most popular means of searching for that special person and nowadays there is absolutely no stigma attached to it.

There are numerous sites offering dating services for the more mature person and it really is up to you to do your research before committing yourself to any one site in particular. Bear in mind that there will be costs involved and that some sites may not always make these costs obvious. Read through the online information available and do your research before making a commitment to use them.

There are also a few basic rules to remember about online dating and most of these are to do with being cautious. When arranging to meet someone for the first time you should make sure that someone else knows where you are going and who you are meeting and it is a good idea to meet in a public place. Also beware of anybody who asks for money as this is likely to be a con.

There is no reason to let these negative thoughts put you off, however, as the vast majority of people using the online site will be as normal as you, so it is just a case of being cautious while you are getting to know somebody.

The good thing about the more mature person you find on an online dating service is that they tend to be more honest about describing themselves and in what they are looking for in a relationship. They are not playing games because they know that this is a serious business for them as well and they are looking for a favourable and beneficial outcome. You undoubtedly have a common goal and do not want to waste your valuable time and money.

Initial contact can often be through an email and then perhaps via skyping, texts and phone calls. Getting to know somebody in this way can not only help avoid mismatching but also help take away some of the nerves about meeting for the first time. Talking about yourselves and sharing information such as your likes and dislikes before actually meeting will quickly let you know if you have common interests. It will also give you something to talk about when you do eventually meet.

Better to take a little time to find these things out rather than rush in and be disappointed. Ultimately, saying no by way of an email or text, is a lot easier than sitting opposite someone and telling them that they are not suitable for you. Dating never was straightforward or easy, as you may vaguely recall, but modern communications systems do make it much easier and take out some of the stress.

### Other opportunities to meet a new partner

Even so, internet dating and partner seeking may still scare the life out of you and therefore may not be suitable. Fortunately this does not mean that there is no chance for you to meet somebody as there are numerous other ways of meeting like-minded people.

If, for example, you fancy a holiday but have nobody to go with, then seek out one of the specialist holiday companies that cater for solo trips. The choice of destinations is enormous and tailored to suit different budgets. So whether it's an exotic trip to the Caribbean, a cruise around the Mediterranean or just a nice summer holiday in your own country, you will find a holiday or tour company who can offer you what you want.

The good thing about a solo holiday is that once again you are going to meet people who are in the same situation as you. They will also be there because they are lonely and while this type of holiday may not find a new life partner for you, it may provide long-term friendships and probably lots of fun along the way.

The experience of meeting new people and having the confidence to talk to them and spend time together is in itself a valuable exercise that can bring renewed confidence and energy to your own outlook on life. Trips and holidays of this type may become a regular event for you because of the benefits and enjoyment they bring.

## Finding new friends by joining in

You may not be seeking a new partner but instead would just like to have some new friends to share some time with. Finding these friends may not be as difficult as you think.

On a local basis there are likely to be numerous opportunities to get together with other people and you will just need to search them out using such sources as the internet, local newspapers and magazines, leaflets at your local doctors' surgery and by talking to friends and neighbours.

For example, there are likely to be many clubs and associations that are always looking out for new members and you will just need to decide what type of activity suits you best. These could be physical exercise groups, including dancing and walking, which are a great way to help stay fit as well as joining a group activity with other people. Even though you may be alone there is no need to be put off from going. Many people go to dancing clubs alone and then pair up with a stranger. After all; nothing ventured, nothing gained!

Or you may be more interested in a hobby or craft group which can be great fun as well as being excellent for stimulating the mind. Enjoying an activity is always enhanced when you can meet and talk with others who share the same enthusiasm for it. You may already have a particular hobby that you want to share within a group but even if you do not then there may be something, in which you would like to get involved for the first time. Exploring and finding new interests is a tremendous way to meet new people and possibly form friendships as well as exercising your own mind and giving you a new interest in life. It is easy sometimes just to continue to do the same old things and the trouble with that is that you can become stale and boring. Try something new and you may be pleasantly surprised with the results it brings and the doors it opens.

From book clubs to star gazing; from line dancing to ballroom sessions; IT clubs to bridge groups, you will find the choice is simply staggering and most of them will cost little to join.

Whatever your preferences, be prepared to give them a try. If you find after a while that they are not for you then it is quite simple to try something else instead. If you are looking for new friendships then the wider you cast the net the more likely you are to reap the benefits. Just keep an open mind and have plenty of fun as you try out different things along the way.

Sitting at home watching TV is not going to do much for your health or stop you from feeling lonely whereas getting out and taking part in something will be good for you.

### Volunteering

In a similar vein, some people often seek new experiences and new friendships by volunteering.

If you have retired from your work or just find yourself with spare time on your hands, voluntary work is an excellent way of forging new relationships to replace the friendships you may have experienced in your previous workplace.

When doing voluntary work you are likely to meet similar people who are also looking to build new friendships and who enjoy meeting new people.

Volunteering has the added benefits of keeping the mind sharp; enjoying totally new experiences and creating the satisfaction of knowing that you are doing something beneficial for a worthwhile cause.

So how do you go about finding out what's available in your area?

Well, again, the internet is a great starting place and there are numerous volunteering websites available for you to browse and see what's available.

Do your research and consider not only the type of things that you would enjoy doing but also the type of work, with which you feel capable of coping.

Whether it be in a charity shop; your local hospital or working outside on a conservation project you are likely to find something that not only suits you but which is also both enjoyable and rewarding.

Working as a volunteer is a great way to put something back into society while also creating great opportunities for you to meet new people and possibly develop relationships.

## Relationships are important

Once you have completed your Relationship Circle and examined the quantity and quality of all the relationships you have you will be in a very well informed position to consider exactly where you are with your relationships. Your thoughts will be based upon real facts and careful consideration rather than emotive feelings.

You will also know whether or not you are missing out on

good friendships. If you feel that you are, you should also, by now, have a better idea what you can do to improve your situation.

If you feel that you are already in a good position then you are very fortunate and it is down to you to continue to nurture and value those relationships. In doing so, make sure that you enjoy all the comfort, support and benefits which they bring to you.

If you do arrive at the decision that you would like to have better friendships then now is the time to get started, using not only the ideas discussed in this chapter, but by every means at your disposal.

Once again it comes down to you putting in the effort and, in doing so, reaping the benefits.

Making The Most Of It is likely to be much more enjoyable and rewarding when you share it with others, for whom you care and who care for you.

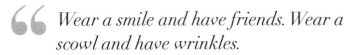 *Wear a smile and have friends. Wear a scowl and have wrinkles.*

George Eliot

◎ If you are feeling lonely and isolated promise yourself to find new friends.

◎ If you are seeking a new partner you need to be bold.

◎ Meeting someone new can be just as daunting for the other person.

◎ Internet dating is easy and safe as long as you follow the basic rules.

◎ Explore all the different ways you can to meet a new partner.

◎ You can make new friends by trying something new and joining in.

◎ Life is a lot more fun with good friends.

# 6.

## ANTI-AGEING – THE WAY YOU LOOK; THE WAY YOU THINK AND BEHAVE

### The Fountain of Youth

 *There is a Fountain of Youth; it is in your mind, your talents, the creativity you bring to your life and the lives of the people you love. When you learn to tap this source you will truly have defeated old age.*

Sophia Loren

The task of holding back age and the restoration of youth has occupied minds for thousands of years. Tales of the Fountain of Youth appear as early as in Greek Legends and in stories of Alexander the Great who crossed the Land of Darkness to find the Fountain.

Over the centuries there have frequently been stories of water with mystical powers in such widespread locations as Ethiopia, India, the Caribbean and the mystical land of Bimini in the western most district of the Bahamas.

The Spanish were very interested in discovering a Fountain of Youth and there exist stories of Conquistadors searching for

71

the magical fountain when they travelled to the Americas in the 16th century.

The home of one enduring and popular legend is to be found in Florida, USA, where the city of St Augustine has long been associated with the fountain and is home to the Fountain of Youth Archaeological Park, which is a popular tourist attraction. Visitors come from around the world to drink from the Fountain in the hope that they can restore their youth. Unfortunately for all of us there is no evidence to date that the water can restore youthfulness.

If a Fountain of Youth truly existed, it would, of course, provide the complete and ultimate answer to the eternal question of how to avoid the ageing process. What an amazing discovery that would be! It would probably also save the enormous amount of money which is spent every year in buying pills, potions, creams and treatments which provide some respite from ageing. Obviously it would be very bad news for the companies that like to sell us all these things.

The appeal is, of course, obvious, after all, who wants to look old? Especially if you are intent on Making The Most Of *It*.

So the age old quest to find the Fountain of Youth continues albeit now in the metaphorical sense as we each try to find our own solution to avoid looking old.

Fortunately the answer probably lays a lot closer to home.

**Finding your own fountain of youth**
The answer to this question is not difficult or mystical and does not involve travelling to far flung destinations to drink from a

fountain, however appealing that may sound! Instead it simply requires you to seriously consider important of aspects of your health and habits.

It really all comes down to how you look; how you physically feel and how mentally alert you are.

## The way you look

Start by taking stock of your own physical appearance. Ask yourself some key questions concerning whether or not you are unnecessarily looking older than you should.

Here are some of the things you should be considering.

Is your hair untidy and badly in need of professional help; does your skin look wrinkled and dull; are your clothes old and unfashionable; do you walk with hunched shoulders?

If the answer to any or all of these is 'Yes', then you need to take some action.

Sometimes it is too easy to neglect your appearance because you cannot be bothered any more or you simply have stopped noticing how you look. This is a sure-fire formula for looking old and indeed for premature ageing. It also makes you unattractive to others so could also be detrimental to your relationships. Ask yourself whether or not you are just being lazy or is it that you just have stopped being aware of what is happening to you?

However, if you want to avoid looking old beyond your years and want to just generally look good, you owe it to yourself to take responsibility for your appearance and start taking some serious and positive self-help action. Lack of money is no real excuse as very simple improvements can be made, which do not involve spending much.

### *Your mental approach and self-esteem are important*

It is much more about your mental approach and the amount of self-pride you have. Looking prematurely old and dowdy can be the mark of lack of self-care. It is a dangerous state to slip into, however, as it can also have a negative psychological effect on you by seriously detracting from your self-esteem and personal confidence. If you look old and shabby it is very hard to feel good about yourself.

By improving your physical appearance you will not only look better but are also likely to feel a lot better and in doing so help towards your goal of Making The Most Of *It*. Walking about with a smile on your face makes you a much more attractive person and a much more interesting one as well.

Start with the simple and easy to do things like a visit to the hairdressers for a smart cut or even maybe a new hair style and, once you have got it looking how you like, make a daily effort to keep it that way. After all it only takes a few minutes.

For men it is also important to keep facial hair under control, to stay looking sharp and to refrain from having hair growing in places you would rather not have it. Out-of-control whiskers, bushy eyebrows and hair growing out of ears and noses can be extremely ageing as well as being decidedly unattractive.

Another highly visible part of your body is your hands; uncared for hands will not only look unsightly but will also age your appearance. Well-manicured hands, for both sexes, can readily be achieved by simple and regular attention and can always be further improved by a visit to a professional manicurist if your budget stretches to it.

These are all straight forward and relatively simple things to do, but are a great starting place to improve your appearance and avoid succumbing to ageing.

### Wrinkled skin is so ageing

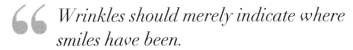 *Wrinkles should merely indicate where smiles have been.*

Mark Twain

Another really important area in the avoidance of appearing agéd is the condition of your skin. In particular, facial skin which is the physical part of you that is on show all the time. Poor facial skin quality will definitely add to the ageing process so it is important that you take action to get your skin looking the best it can be.

Good skin quality will result primarily from a healthy lifestyle involving what you eat and drink, whether or not you exercise and whether you over expose your skin to the elements. It will also benefit enormously from the care you give to your skin by cleansing and moisturising.

The way your skin looks is frequently a good indicator of how well you are doing internally so having good skin is not just a question of looking better.

So what type of things do you have to watch out for that will damage your skin?

A major factor is excess free radicals in the body which will accelerate ageing process. These can be caused by too much exposure to the sun; air pollution; pesticides and even too much use of your mobile phone. These excess free radicals will break down your vital DNA defences and trigger deterioration, damaging cells throughout your body.

The body does have built in defence mechanisms to help clean up these molecules but you can help yourself by making sure that your daily diet includes food rich in the antioxidant vitamins A, C and E. If you need help in identifying which foods you should eat which are rich in these vitamins you can consult your Doctor or find suitable internet sites which will explain this.

Externally caring for your skin is also important and you should use products which are rich in Vitamin A derivatives and Vitamin C. Vitamin A targets wrinkles and helps to regulate the skin functions which are known to slow down with age.

Vitamin C is important in the production of collagen which is the key protein in the skin that provides its flexibility. We often associate wrinkled skin with age so the flexibility will help avoid this happening.

As you will already be aware the market is full of skin care products and each one is 'guaranteed' to make you look more youthful. Although this vast choice may be bewildering it is really a case of finding what works for you and is within your budget.

Remember, though, that what you put in your body is just as important as what you put on it, so make sure that your diet is really healthy too.

Another essential for good looking skin is to make sure you stay well hydrated by drinking plenty of water throughout the day. You should also take care to avoid foods which cause the skin to look bloated. This results from eating high carb foods as well as salty and sugary snacks. They can all cause fluid to be retained in the body and result in facial bloating.

### Relax your mind and body

Mind relaxing physical exercises such as yoga, Pilates and tai chi are all useful in combating the ageing process and keeping skin healthy. Aerobic exercises are great to help you keep fit and alert but a mindfulness approach really helps connect you with your body and can be done virtually anywhere and at any time.

Facial yoga is an increasingly popular exercise to tone the muscles in the face leaving your skin with a youthful glow.

Try it for yourself by pulling a massive wide open smile while avoiding wrinkling around your eyes. Turn the corners of your lips up as far as they will go and feel the cheeks plump. Or pucker your lips as tight as they will go and try to smile at the same time, holding either of these for about twenty seconds.

These exercises really work the muscles and are easy to do anywhere at any time. You may, however, get a few odd looks if you are in a public place so be careful!

Another major factor in our daily lives which can cause our skin to age is stress. Body ageing results when telomeres, which are the microscopic ends of our DNA that act like bookends to our chromosomes, become too short through repeated cell division. While antioxidant vitamins help prevent damage by free radicals, which also damage and break down our cells, even greater damage is done to these cells by stress. So trying your best to avoid stress is a really important factor in determining how quickly your skin ages.

We have already considered stress in our lives in an earlier chapter and it really is an important consideration in not only enjoying your life but also in anti-ageing. There are many ways of helping avoid the symptoms of stress in the short term such as relaxation and breathing exercises and these can help. However, in the long-term it can only be dealt with by identifying the cause of the stress and, if possible, dealing with the problem.

### Healthy eating is important

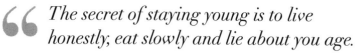

> *The secret of staying young is to live honestly, eat slowly and lie about you age.*
>
> Lucille Ball

When it comes to eating, the rules basically never change, whatever your age. At all times in life, a balanced and healthy diet will help to maintain your health and energy levels and, importantly, keep weight under control thus avoiding illnesses which arise from obesity.

These are all important areas for each of us to watch out for as we get older as it seems ridiculous to make matters worse than they need be simply because we are not careful with our daily diet.

There are some very simple rules to follow such as trying to eat a diet which includes:

◎ Plenty of fruit and vegetables every day
◎ A handful of unsalted nuts
◎ Starchy foods such as rice, bread, potatoes and pasta
◎ A limited amount of milk and dairy foods
◎ Some meat, fish, eggs and beans to give you protein. Oily fish is particularly good for you.

Apart from what you should eat it is also a good idea to avoid too much consumption of foods and drinks that are high in fat or sugar.

These simple rules may make the daily task of eating healthier sound boring but it is the way food is prepared that takes away the blandness, so a good cook book (or a good cook!) always comes in handy.

Just be careful in adding too many pre-prepared sauces as these are often high in ingredients such as salt which are not too good for you. The same goes for processed meats and pre-prepared meals.

### What healthy foods do for you and your body

For a start, foods rich in starch and fibre are very good for your digestion and help avoid constipation and other digestive problems.

Foods rich in iron help maintain and restore energy levels. We all need more energy as we age, particularly if we intend to pursue an active life.

Calcium rich foods helps keep your bones healthy and can help you to avoid osteoporosis which is when the density of your bones decreases. Keeping bones healthy avoids the risk of fractures which is always an area of concern as age increases.

Eat less salt, ensuring that you consume less than six grams per day. Salt can raise you blood pressure and increase the risks of health problems such as heart diseases or a stroke. Once you stop using salt you will soon find that you no longer like the taste in your food.

Unfortunately, salt is used frequently, and often excessively, in the pre-prepared foods we buy, so it is often difficult to know how much you are consuming. To avoid this you can carefully read the labels on food to check contents, but a safer way is to prepare fresh foods yourself and avoid adding extra salt.

Make sure you also get enough vitamin D in your diet as it aids healthy bones by helping you to absorb calcium. Vitamin D comes from exposure to sunshine but you should also try and get it through the foods that you eat.

For each of these items the best way to research how to get the right foods to help you is by a simple search on the internet. However, as a basic rule it is better to eat fresh foods that you prepare yourself (rather than processed foods) and mix your food types to achieve a healthy balance.

### *Unhealthy eating has unhealthy consequences*

To Make The Most Of *It*, you need a healthy body and a healthy mind and diet is a major contributor to being able to live the life you want as you grow older. The consequences of unhealthy eating should not be underestimated.

If you are overweight you may find yourself becoming less mobile which in turn can seriously affect your health and your quality of life. The risk of illnesses such as diabetes and heart disease increases significantly.

Being underweight can also be a problem and can increase the risk of osteoporosis. It may be that you are not eating enough or not eating a balanced diet but either way you should get it checked out to ensure that it is not a sign that you have something wrong with you.

Sometimes as we get older our appetite can decrease, particularly if we become less active, and interest in food can decline.

The answer to this is to eat less at each meal but eat more often, perhaps supplementing meals with healthy snacks

An essential element of your diet and good health is avoiding dehydration. You should try to drink at least 1.2 litres of fluid every day. Most types of drinks count towards this total but if the drink contains too much caffeine it will act as a diuretic and will have the opposite of the required effect. The healthiest choice is water but if you do not fancy drinking that much water every day try decaffeinated drinks or add a little natural fruit juice to your water.

As you may well have realised by now it is all down to

understanding what you are doing with your food and drink intake and then making the choices you believe are correct for you and your health. Healthy eating and drinking need to be positive lifestyle choices and not something you switch on and off as your mood changes. Establish a healthy routine and then stick to it.

There is an abundance of medical evidence available which clearly indicates that a healthy and balanced diet gives you a far greater chance of not only living longer but also staying fitter and healthier along the way and in doing so making you look and feel better.

The ageing effects of poor health caused by poor diet can normally be avoided but you have to make the choice and take the positive steps necessary.

The choice, as always, is yours.

### The way you dress

The speed at which fashions change is staggering and is driven by the constant efforts of the fashion industry and clothes retailers to create fresh demand. This is demand which is stimulated in the shopper by changes in fashion rather than the basic need for something to wear. We are convinced by clever advertising that we must keep abreast of the latest designs, shapes and colours so that we avoid looking outdated and unfashionable.

It is a massive, worldwide industry and we are constantly aware of it through the expensive advertising and marketing campaigns which are pushed at us daily on a multi-media basis.

Often movie or sports stars are used to promote major brands knowing that many consumers will seek to emulate these famous and glamorous people.

The good news though, is that the latest fashion is no longer reserved for the wealthy because department stores, catalogue and online retailers have introduced a huge choice of up to the minute clothing at budget prices. In doing so they have made the very latest fashions available to most people and you no longer have to pay a fortune to own them. They have created and brought into the market clothes at a price which you can afford to wear, and then dispose of, once you get bored with them.

Of course there still exists high quality clothing which will last and which relies less on current fashion and more on what is termed 'classic' styling. It can look very good on the right person but costs a lot more in the first place. It is likely to be worn regardless of changes in fashion.

What this means overall though is that whatever your budget, there is likely to be something out there that is affordable. With this in mind when you choose what you wear there is often no need to dress yourself in clothing which ages you.

If you have resolved to Make The Most Of *It,* then making the best of the way you look is highly relevant to avoid looking aged.

For you to successfully use clothes to help you look good you need to avoid badly fitting clothes, fashions which are clearly out-dated, colours which do not suit you and clothing which is associated with being old.

If you are unsure as to what a person of your age should be wearing to still look stylish there are plenty of places to get ideas. Have a good browse through some catalogues or online shopping sites or simply look through newspapers and magazines. There is always plenty to choose from. Once you have done so you can identify the types and styles of clothing that will suit your body shape and your personality as well as your pocket.

You are definitely not trying to look like a teenager again, because those days are well and truly gone, but neither do you want to look like an old fogey!

All you are doing is simply making the most of who you are and as result you will not only look good but also feel better. Being nicely dressed creates a wonderful boost to your confidence and self-esteem. Feeling good about yourself and the way you look is a great feeling.

Just remember, it is not a question of spending a lot of money. It is more about being aware of how you look and taking a little time to choose what is right for you. If you are unsure what suits you best you might consider asking your partner or a friend for their opinion.

## The way you think and behave
### *Exercising the mind*
One of the great fears associated with ageing is the diminishing mental capabilities that can gradually occur.

As we grow older we can sometimes experience a decline in our ability to stay focused and to think clearly and quickly.

We may also be aware of a deteriorating ability to remember. This can cause frustration and occasionally embarrassment, particularly when it comes to forgetting names.

We should all be aware that this can happen to any one of us. Equally we should also be aware, that as far as this aspect of ageing is concerned, there are many things we can do about it.

Consider the brain like a muscle in your body and as you will know, muscles need to be exercised to keep them functional and healthy. The same applies to your brain and the adage 'Use it or lose it' is highly relevant.

In your younger years you may have been working or bringing up a family and every day your brain would have been fully occupied just in the task of coping with everything going on your life. In addition, you may have been studying or learning new skills or pursuing hobbies and interests which kept your mind constantly engaged and active. In other words, your brain was constantly working and being exercised.

At the age of sixty many of these situations may no longer exist in your daily life and you may find yourself in the situation where your brain not only begins to relax but also becomes under-employed. By not working it so hard the capabilities of your brain will begin to diminish and as a consequence the sharpness of your mind will suffer. Just like the muscles in your body which deteriorate with lack of exercise, the brain also begins to deteriorate and no longer functions as well as it once did.

Not the most pleasant of thoughts for any of us!

So the answer for most people is relatively straightforward

and just requires you to make that choice to do something about it. Best to do this while you can still remember to do so.

Keeping mentally alert and having a sharp focus will be of enormous benefit to you in your personal anti-ageing campaign and will be fundamental in your desire to Make The Most Of *It*.

### Find the right way for you to sharpen up your brain

There are a number of ways to do this and if you start by making a list of your own ideas you will be surprised at all the suggestions you can come up with.

You can try regularly doing puzzles, crosswords and number games such as Sudoku, and if you do them regularly set yourself time challenges to make you even sharper.

Games such as chess and scrabble are also wonderful for getting the brain cells stimulated; and pursuing whatever other hobbies and interests you have will also benefit and exercise your brain.

However, one of the best and simplest ways to keep the brain stimulated and sharp is to have good, active conversations with people. Add to this a good dose of laughter and you will activate your ventromedial prefrontal cortex where dopamine is released into your body. Dopamine plays an important part in developing cognition, learning, memory and attention.

The really important thing for you is to identify actions and activities which you want to do and then get on and do them. This will help keep you mentally alert and also be enormously enjoyable as well so the benefits are substantial.

A further means of developing the brain, that many use, is

meditation. The thought of spending time meditating is not going to suit everyone and you may prefer a more active route to stimulate your mind. However, meditating is believed to have the power to bring about permanent structural changes to your brain for the better. Studies have shown that those who use meditation to clear their minds and focus their thoughts have bigger brains and experience fewer neuron losses and even have a reduced rate of white matter tissue decline than others of a similar age.

Whatever you decide is best for you to keep your brain alert and sharp will be your choice but you need to be aware that if you want to keep your mind ticking and be as bright as a button then you need to take action.

No-one wants to reach that point when people in the same room are talking about you as though you do not exist, believing you to be incapable of participating in the conversation.

### Habits that age us

Throughout our lives we develop habits, some good and some bad. The ones you need to watch out for as you reach sixty are those that are particularly associated with ageing.

These could include things like failing asleep every afternoon, repeating yourself when you speak; driving your car at a snail's pace; sighing every time you sit down; wanting to go to bed at the same time every night; complaining about the weather to everyone you meet and talking continuously about your health to anyone who will listen.

Do any of these strike a chord with you or do you have your own habits that you could add to the list? Think about it for a moment and you might begin to identify habits that you have developed in your own more mature years.

Until now you may not even be aware that you have developed these habits and you certainly will not be aware that in the eyes of others they are making you seem old.

If you continue with these habits you can be sure that you will be considered old by those who witness them and the longer these habits go unchecked the more likely they are to become permanent features of your personality.

To be successful in your anti-ageing efforts you need to stop and think about your habits or if you have the courage, ask someone who is close to you to help identify them for you. This may initially be embarrassing and may even surprise you but it is better to find out sooner rather than later so that you can do something about it. You may need a thick skin to listen to what they have to say because it will be easy to think that they are criticising you.

### Overcoming ageing habits

Once you have discovered, either by yourself or with the help of others, any unfortunate ageing habits you have developed, the next steps are to avoid repeating them in the future and to develop new and better habits to replace them.

For example, rather than taking a comfortable nap every afternoon, which becomes extremely habit forming, try going for a nice brisk walk instead. As you walk, practise mindfulness of the moment, and instead of thinking about things that have happened or worrying about tomorrow, absorb yourself in the sights, smells, sounds and colours – becoming conscious of all that is around you.

You will find this wonderfully relaxing and stress-free as well as being good aerobic exercise bringing benefits to the mind as well as the body. You will return energised and refreshed and will find that the afternoon nap is no longer required.

If you find yourself doing the same thing every day then make a conscious effort to be more unpredictable. It will be stimulating for you and make you more interesting to others.

To those who know you the difference will be readily apparent and it will contribute to your efforts to avoid the effects of ageing.

It is so easy to reflect our age in the way we act and behave. It is true for children as much as it is for the sixty-year-old and will soon be spotted by those people with whom we come into regular contact. If you want to help avoid the ageing process in yourself and avoid others thinking you are old, checking and correcting your habits will make a big difference.

## Can you discover your own fountain of youth?

You should be aware by now that the ageing process can be slowed down significantly if you are prepared to look after yourself and be aware of how you act and behave.

There is no magical Fountain of Youth – well not one that produces the desired results – so as with most things in life, it comes down to self-help.

If you want to hold back the years, look good, feel even better, then it is all within your power to do so, by tapping into your own willpower rather than the fountain.

After all, who amongst us wants to look old when you have a choice?

Who still wants to Make The Most Of *It*?

Start your anti-ageing plan today!

 *Age is strictly a case of mind over matter. If you don't mind, it doesn't matter."*

Jack Benny

---

**MEMORY JOGGERS**

- ◎ The magical Fountain of Youth remains undiscovered.
- ◎ Sharpen up your physical appearance to avoid looking out of date.
- ◎ Boost your self-esteem by taking pride in how you look.
- ◎ What you put in your body is equally as important as what you put on it.
- ◎ Dress to impress.
- ◎ Clear out of your wardrobe all old and ill-fitting clothes.
- ◎ Exercise your brain to keep it active and alert.
- ◎ Check out your habits and dump the age related ones.

# 7.

## SEX AT SIXTY

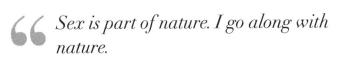 *Sex is part of nature. I go along with nature.*

Marilyn Munroe

For those who are much younger, it may come as a bit of a shock, and also possibly raise a few sniggers that any old codger at the age of sixty could possibly still have a sex life.

To imagine your parents at that decrepit age still indulging in sex would be quite unthinkable and probably repulsive to a younger person. Fortunately that decision does not rest with your children or anybody else but you.

There is no reason why our sex drive and the desire for a physically intimate relationship should not last all our lives. After all there are no rules or laws governing the age at which participating in sex should cease.

We are all born with natural instincts to look after ourselves and our families and to perpetuate human life. We eat, drink, sleep and reproduce as an essential part of our on-going existence. Participation in sexual activity is inborn in us and is entirely natural behaviour which has perpetuated mankind and although this instinct may wane somewhat with age, it certainly does not disappear.

Why should it? True, the passion may not be as strong as it was when you were younger and there are a number of reasons why this is the case. However, for most sixty-year-olds, sexual desire will still be there and it needs to be considered as still an important aspect of your life.

If you want to Make The Most Of *It* from sixty onwards, then a healthy sex life should definitely be included in your plans for the future.

## Consider the benefits of regular sex

While sex is highly pleasurable, there are also a number of other benefits which result from it which you may not have even thought about before. This is quite normal because probably the last thing on your mind when indulging in sexual activity is, 'What other benefits am I getting out of this?' Your mind is probably otherwise occupied!

When the mood strikes there is usually only one thought for both parties.

However, these are some of the suggested benefits that sex can bring for you:

◎ It can help to relieve stress and anxiety
◎ It can help to boost your immune system
◎ Sex is good for the heart
◎ It burns calories and helps keep weight down
◎ Good sex can greatly boost your self-esteem as well as that of your partner

- Sex helps create a closer bond with your partner
- For the male, regular sex may help to reduce the risk of prostate cancer
- There is a good chance that following sex you will sleep better

These 'add-on' benefits are obviously worth enjoying as bonus side-effects from a pleasurable activity that is good for both you and your partner.

## Loss of libido

The drawback is, however, that with age, and also in the case of long-term relationships, the passion can wane and sex can become infrequent or possibly stop altogether. Perhaps an easier way to describe it is that it becomes boring – and once that happens it is easy to lose interest.

It should be remembered that, as you grow older, the loss of your sex drive can easily occur as a natural process and if you and your partner are both happy with your relationship involving less sex then that is entirely up to you.

For many, though, it can be a frustrating and worrying experience resulting in concern, anxiety and even distress for one or both parties. It can also put a strain on relationships. To help deal with these feelings the first step is to try and understand why this is happening.

It may not be straightforward; the reasons for loss of libido can be many and varied. In some cases there may be an obvious explanation but in others it may be much more complicated.

Not knowing why or understanding what is happening can naturally be very stressful for the individual.

Trying to deal with this issue by yourself is only likely to put more strain on you. The best course of action to avoid this happening may be to seek help from your doctor who is initially the best informed person to give you guidance and advice. Your doctor can help you better identify and understand the cause of the problem and how it can best be rectified. Whilst you may feel hesitant about raising such a personal issue with your doctor, be assured that they will have almost certainly encountered this matter many times before.

If, however, you still feel that it is not something that you can discuss with them but still want to deal with this issue, an alternative is to try and research the problem further for yourself.

Many websites cover loss of libido but an excellent source of information is the NHS Choices site. This gives a detailed explanation of why the sex drive can be affected and what the possible causes may be. Issues covered include relationship issues; stress, anxiety and exhaustion; depression; drugs and alcohol; hormonal problems; medical conditions and medication. Importantly, it also discusses the effect of ageing on libido

Not only does this website give you a much greater insight into the causes of a loss of sex drive, it also gives useful recommendations as to how tackle the problem.

Whatever you decide is the best way to deal with this matter, if it affects you, the important point is that you do get on and deal with it. Otherwise it will continue to cause you emotional distress and will seriously affect your happiness.

You may believe that the loss of libido in your own relationship is simply down to familiarity and boredom. It is not the case that you no longer love your partner or even find them unattractive. The loss of passion is just down to the fact that you have been together a long time and your sex life has become stale and routine. Like so many other aspects of our lives, the same routine day in and day out will quite naturally create boredom.

To help restore the excitement and passion back to your love life and to help make it more successful and fulfilling for both parties, there are things that you can try. As always, you will have to make a bit of an effort if you are to Make The Most Of *It*.

Excitement and passion are generated by the thoughts you have and if your thoughts about sex are so boring that you fail to generate these feelings then you need to do something about it. You may be wondering how you can go about changing these negative thoughts so here are a few suggestions.

## Tips to help restore your libido and get your sex life back on track

### Communication

A great place to start is to try and discuss your sex life with your partner. It really is amazing how people who have been together for many years and who have regularly experienced sex together, have never actually discussed it. It may be embarrassment or the fear of offending your partner, but while you could both be having lots of thoughts about sex, or the lack of it, in your relationship, you never actually discuss it.

You may be able to talk about all sorts of aspects of your life together but sex is off the list. For some reason it has become a taboo topic, about which you are both aware, but do not speak.

So now is the time to connect on this issue. Introduce the subject gently and try to engage your partner in an open discussion rather than just expressing your own thoughts. Listen to what your partner has to say. You may find that for both of you the relief of being able to discuss your own feelings and to understand those of your partner is a great therapeutic process that will bring you closer together.

## Routine

One of the reasons why sexual activity can dwindle is the boredom of making love in the same place, at the same time and in the same way. As with most things in life we easily get bored with routine. Imagine eating the same food for lunch every day or watching the same movie night after night. You would soon get bored and start making changes to make your life more interesting.

Exactly the same principle should apply to your sex life. Stop doing exactly the same thing and try something different. There is no need to go extremely different as you and your partner may feel uncomfortable with this so 'gently does it' is the best way. For example, if you always have sex in the same bed in the same room try making love somewhere else. If you usually only make love at night, try a daytime session or first thing in the morning. Try different lighting in your bedroom or go to bed naked. Whatever you decide just try and create a bit more excitement for both of you. You could be pleasantly surprised at the difference this makes to your levels of desire.

### Too tired

After a busy day, maybe working or looking after the grandchildren, or coping with all the household chores, the last thing you probably feel interested in is sex. Understandably so, as we all get tired both physically and mentally and the only thing you want is a cup of hot chocolate and a good night's sleep. The problem is that if all your days are like this and you are constantly busy, busy, busy you will always feel tired and not have the time or the energy to engage in sex.

The answer to this problem is a relatively simple one as you simply need to plan time for you and your partner to be together, just by yourselves. You could set aside an evening when just the two of you can go out for a meal or simply stay at home and watch a movie together, maybe sharing a bottle of wine. Relax together and enjoy each other's company with no-one butting in or asking you to do something. Just enjoy being together and enjoying each other's company, creating a feeling of closeness and intimacy that is not always possible. Round off the evening by enjoying sex together and sleep soundly afterwards. It simply takes a little planning and setting the time aside.

### Romance

Romance is that exciting quality which can slowly disappear in a relationship. If you can reignite romance between you and your partner, a better sex life should result.

Partners frequently take each other for granted, particularly in long term relationships. Romance becomes replaced by complacency and ignoring the feelings of your partner.

Consider, for a moment, the early days of your courtship and the romance that existed between you. Remember the loving gestures you made to each other and the exciting feelings those gestures created.

It is likely that if you compare those days to how you behave towards each other now you may realise that there is a stark contrast. Naturally it is difficult to maintain romance at the level it was in the early days of your relationship, but has it disappeared altogether?

Only you and your partner will be able to answer that question.

If you recognise that a loss of romance is an issue in your relationship which has contributed to a decline in your sex life then you should consider making changes.

If both of you take a genuine interest in each other and make an effort to keep romance alive in your relationship it is bound to have a beneficial effect on your sex life.

As with everything in life, the more effort you put in, the more likely you are to reap the rewards.

If putting the fizz and passion back into your sex life is firmly part of your plans to Make The Most Of *It*, now is the time to give some serious consideration to your own circumstances and how you can go about it.

We often 'make do' or put up with situations because we

have got into a rut and become complacent about things. If you feel that this has happened to you and has affected your sex life, then take this as a wake-up call. You have a lot of life ahead of you but at the same time you cannot afford to waste a moment more of it. Take control and instead of mourning the loss of passion and excitement in your life start taking action to revive it. The chances are you will be delighted with the results!

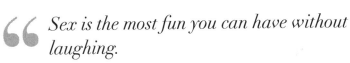 *Sex is the most fun you can have without laughing.*

Woody Allen

---

## MEMORY JOGGERS

- ◎ Our sex drive is a natural instinct. It is the passion, which wanes.
- ◎ Regular sex is not just enjoyable – it is also good for your health.
- ◎ Loss of libido can be different for everyone and may need an individual approach to restore it.
- ◎ Get professional help if it does not cause you embarrassment to do so.
- ◎ Improve your libido by talking about sex with your partner and overcoming boredom.
- ◎ Restore the romance and make time for sex.

# 8.

## ACHIEVING YOUR AMBITIONS

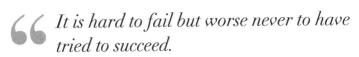 *It is hard to fail but worse never to have tried to succeed.*

Theodore Roosevelt

A large proportion of every individual's life is spent in simply fulfilling the basic needs and necessities of their existence. This is time spent working to earn money to provide for the things we need, learning, exercising, cooking and eating, doing household chores, looking after children and other needy people, sleeping, shopping, etc., etc., etc.. The list goes on and on and you are probably all too familiar with it.

These basic needs and necessities can often take up all of our time and leave little room for pursuing our ambitions and aspirations which may become merely a dream rather than reality. Even if a spare moment does present itself to you, there is the chance that you will be too exhausted to take much advantage of it. This may all sound familiar to you.

Life has become increasingly like this with constant demands on our time and energy leaving little room even to consider loftier ambitions let alone pursue them. In many ways this is why so many people idolise famous sports personalities and pop and movie stars because they present an opportunity to identify with a lifestyle that the individual knows that they will never be able to achieve for themselves. By reading about these people and following them on social media sites there is the chance to share in some of their glamorous and exciting lifestyles.

It can frequently happen that by the time we reach sixty we may feel that we have not truly done all the things we wanted to do with our lives, leaving us with a feeling of dissatisfaction and being unfulfilled. This can create deep dissatisfaction inside us and even anger because we know that time is not on our side.

This can quite easily happen because we all have a hierarchy of needs in our life, which starts at its most basic with the need to look after ourselves and our families. Thus we take steps to feed and clothe ourselves and to keep warm and safe. Once we have fulfilled those needs we can then start to consider the other needs that we have in our lives which may involve finding a partner or our careers and skills development. Having achieved those we are then in a position to consider our real aspirational desires that we have floating about in our minds.

Unfortunately a progressive and logical procession through satisfying all these needs is rarely achieved. Some basic needs may be more difficult to achieve than we anticipated because of our prevailing circumstances. Sometimes we may be well on our way to satisfying all our needs when something happens and we slip backwards. You could lose your job, split from your partner or discover a baby is on the way. There are so many unexpected events that may happen which can upset your plans and throw your life into confusion.

All of a sudden your hierarchy of needs will dictate that you have to get these things sorted out again before you can even consider your more aspirational desires. This is why so many dreams and ambitions are never actually achieved during our younger years.

If you are aware that this happened to you and you are still harbouring those same dreams and ambitions then you need to Make The Most Of It and take action now. There certainly is still time to do all those things you have always wanted, but have never quite got around to achieving.

## What are your unsatisfied ambitions?

If you still want to desperately achieve something in your life and there is something you really want to do, then it remains an important aspiration for you and you can still do something about it.

We are all likely to have had many burning ambitions throughout our lives as we strive to achieve and fulfil our potential to the maximum. Some people are more ambitious than others and sometimes being over ambitious can cause unnecessary stress and, potentially, disappointment for the individual if failure is the end result. However, the risk is usually worth taking if you really want the true satisfaction of achievement.

For most of us, at all times in our lives, it is good to have ambitions and aspirations that we want to pursue. Things you want to do, goals you want to achieve, places you want to see, hopes you want to fulfil and a desire to fill your life to capacity with achievement and success. Remember that our lives are not pre-scripted for us so there is absolutely no reason why you cannot choose what you want to do at any time in your life. The decision rests entirely with you. It is important to adopt a positive attitude of doing what you can, with what you have, wherever you might be.

These ambitions give us a reason to get up every day and to strive to fulfil them, however big or small they might be. They give us something to look forward to, hope when things are not so good and great pleasure when we achieve them. They create within us a natural motivation that gets our adrenaline surging and energises our lives.

Once we achieve them the feeling of self-satisfaction is wonderful and great for our self-confidence. It helps us maintain a positive attitude in every other aspect of our lives.

Naturally, we will all have had our own choices of ambitions and aspirations and many of these will have changed over time. Some will have been fulfilled along the way and others will have changed as we go through life and our circumstances alter.

We should also remember that the ambitions we have are not solely meant to be a test of our resolve or our ability to achieve that ambition. No-one is going to criticise you if, ultimately, you have tried but failed to achieve what you set out to do. Do not let fear be an obstacle for you. Look upon your ambitions and aspirations instead, as something that will bring you pleasure, a sense of achievement, fulfilment and a feeling of satisfaction. Your ambitions are chosen by you and are personal to you and if you try, but occasionally fail, to achieve something you wanted to do, no-one can justly criticise you.

What is really important is that it is always better to have tried to fulfil your ambitions rather than just dreaming about them. Remember, Isaac Newton proved that every action has an opposite and equal reaction, so on that basis, the amount of effort you put into realising your ambitions should be rewarded by the amount of success you ultimately achieve. Do nothing and it is likely that nothing will happen as a result! Conversely, the harder you try, the more likely you are to be successful!

So at the age of sixty, is it the time to be considering new ambitions or rekindling old ones? Or is it time to sit back, relax, and be content with all that life has brought up to that point?

Let it be clear that if you are content and satisfied with your life and have no further ambitions then there is nothing wrong with that. You are free to make your own decisions. Peace of mind as opposed to the possibility of self-imposed demands and pressures has a lot going for it and can avoid stress and disappointment.

## Taking practical steps to achieve your ambitions

However, if your approach to Making The Most Of It includes achieving unfulfilled or even new, ambitions and aspirations then perhaps life will be more exciting and rewarding as you set about doing so. With an ever increasing life expectancy of at least another twenty years after the age of sixty, there is still a great deal of time. There are likely to be plenty of things out there that you have never quite got around to doing that you can now really have a try at.

Earlier on in Chapter Two, we looked at making changes in your life and how this could be achieved by drawing up a plan to clarify the desired goals you had established.

When you consider your ambitions and aspirations the process is similar. This time, however, your plans are not so much based on the desire or need to make changes in areas of your life that you feel are not as good as they could be. This time the plans you make are based on the desire to add to your life and achieve something new. Something new that you have an ardent and burning longing to do but have never had the time or opportunity to fulfil, before now.

It is very much up to you, and you alone, to decide what your ambitions and aspirations are for the future. A notepad will come in very handy once again as you begin to think about them. Jot the ideas down as they come into your head and gradually build up a list of your ambitions and the things you still aspire to do. The list may become quite long but there will be plenty of time to sift through it and fully consider where your priorities lie.

As you gradually draw up your list you will probably realise that ambitions can come in all shapes and forms and may not be confined just to yourself but also possibly include your partner and family, if you have one.

Once you have your starting list you will need to put it into some sort of order to help you sort out and clarify your own thoughts about your ambitions. It is a useful idea to group your ambitions under different headings so that you can think more clearly about them before you embark on the pursuit of any of them.

For example you could classify them into groups like this:

## Time classification

Some ambitions will naturally take longer than others to achieve so you might like to group them into time periods such as short term (three months); medium term (twelve months) and longer term (greater than twelve months). With any ambition you embark on it is always a good idea to be aware of how long you anticipate it will take you to achieve it, so that you can monitor your progress along the way.

## Category classification

You can choose your own category headings but they might be areas such as travel; career; educational and skills; family; leisure and sports pursuits; literature and the arts; charity and helping others.

The list of categories can be drawn up to suit your own individual areas of interest.

If you want to pursue more than one ambition at a time you may find it more interesting not to have them too similar to each other. For example if you want to travel to several special places that you have always wanted to visit, it may be better to only plan one trip at a time.

## Difficulty classification

Obviously, some ambitions are going to be, by varying degrees, much more difficult than others to fulfil. For example, to learn a foreign language is likely to be much more time consuming and challenging than visiting a country you have always wanted to go to. It is therefore relevant to take this into consideration when listing your ambitions as you will want to avoid taking on too many difficult things at the same time. You could use a simple grading such as A for very difficult, B hard, C challenging, D relatively easy.

Once you have made a list of your ambitions and classified them by time, type and difficulty you will have a lot clearer idea of the ambitions you have and whether they are all achievable or not.

If your list is a long one you may also at this time start to prioritise them according to the order, in which you want to pursue them. In doing so you can take into consideration the classifications you have allocated to each one. Thus, you may not want to take on more than one long-term ambition at a time or more than one which is going to be difficult to achieve. After all, you are supposed to be enjoying them along the way.

Equally, you can take into account the category for your ambitions as you may not want to pursue more than one ambition which is too similar to another, at the same time.

So what are your ambitions and aspirations? What do you really want to do or achieve to Make The Most Of *It*?

## Identify your ambitions
### *Travel*
Many people have a desire to travel more as they grow older and potentially have more time and a greater opportunity to do so. It is easy to understand why, with the chance to see far off

places that you have never seen before and experience new cultures. The world may be huge yet it is growing smaller everyday with long distance travelling becoming common place. Also it presents a chance, if you so desire, to follow the sun and enjoy warmer weather particularly during the cold season in your home location. What you save on the heating costs for your home will also help pay for your holiday!

Travel is also good for leaving behind the housework and the monotonous routine of daily living. Doing something different for a while is a good way to refresh the body and mind. Having someone else cook your meals, make your bed and clean your room for you gives you more time to relax and enjoy yourself. It is a great opportunity to meet new people, experience lifestyles you have never experienced before and generally have good fun.

Of course there is expense involved and you will need to see if you have the spare money available. Taking the opportunity of out of season deals is a good way to keep the cost down as well as avoiding the crowds.

### Learning something new

For some, having more time in your life also presents a great opportunity for learning something new. Perhaps a new skill or hobby or, for some, educational learning in a subject that interests them. Learning something new in this way can be a tremendous challenge in your later years, yet in doing so it can give you a new perspective on life that you may not have expected. It can take you out of your comfort zone, challenge you, surprise you and be a conduit to new friendships and relationships that you would not have experienced otherwise.

There exist many, many opportunities for learning something new and you can search them out either on a national basis, involving distance learning, or locally where you live. Some may involve a cost which you will need to make sure that you can afford but there will be others that are free or involve a minimal cost. If you are unsure what you want to do, you can always try something before fully committing yourself but for many it will be a long-term, burning ambition that they will stick at and achieve.

### Physical achievements

Maybe your ambitions are not about learning but more about physical achievements such as running a marathon, climbing a mountain, doing a recognised walk, flying in a helicopter or sailing across the South Pacific (not necessarily by yourself). There is just so much to choose from and so many different challenges. As long as you feel capable of the physical challenge then there is no reason why you should not have a go and satisfy that desire. Just think of the reply you will be able to give when a friend asks if you have been doing anything interesting lately!

### Emotional ambitions

Of course, your ambitions may be quite more emotional for you and not involve new challenges. It may be that you just want to spend more time with your partner; playing with the grandchildren or seeing more of your friends. These things are likely to bring you emotional satisfaction and contentment and cost little more than your time and energy.

For others finding time for relaxation and peace of mind after a life time of working hard and strenuously is a worthy ambition.

Whatever your choice, Making The Most Of *It* in terms of ambitions and aspirations is a very important part of having a fulfilling life from sixty onwards and should not be ignored.

## Monitoring your progress

Pursuing your ambitions and aspirations needs to be pleasurable as well as challenging and can be done at your own pace.

For some however, it will be important to set themselves a reasonable time scale to achieve what they want to do, as otherwise it can be too easy to put things off and then it takes longer than you expected in the first place and begins to impinge on other aspects of your life.

If this happens you may also find that pursuing your ambition begins to become a chore rather than a pleasure and this can only end in disappointment.

So whatever it is you set out to achieve it is generally a good idea to put a timetable together for doing so.

For example, if you want to visit a country you have always longed to see, decide well in advance when you are going and start saving and preparing for that date. By making the commitment you are much more likely to make it happen.

If you want to run a marathon then you will also need to decide well in advance where and when that will be and then prepare your plan to work towards that date. This would likely involve your registration and training plans, dietary needs, equipment requirements, travel plans and so on. You can then monitor your progress along the way to ensure that you are on schedule to be ready.

If you want to learn a new subject or skill then you need to prepare by picking the right course or training centre and finding out how long it will take you and what commitment you will have to give. You can also find out about the costs involved to ensure that they are within your budget. It is a good idea to have a sound idea of how long it is going to take you to complete your training and what level of skill you will have achieved. You will then know well in advance how you should be progressing along the way and be able compare your actual progress at timely intervals to ensure all is going to plan.

If with any of your ambitions you find along the way that you are just not making the progress you expected it will be time to take stock and give full consideration as to whether you are going to be able to achieve what you set out to do.

You may find that the time commitment is far greater than you expected or it just more difficult than you anticipate and you are struggling to succeed. It may be more costly than you thought or you may even have started to realise that it was not a suitable ambition for you in the first place. By monitoring your progress along the way you will know if any such situation is occurring, in which case you have a choice. You can continue with what you are doing but make some adjustments to make it easier to achieve your ambition or alternatively, give it up and try something different.

Hopefully, however, you will have planned properly by choosing carefully what you wanted to do from the outset. In addition you will have decided how and when you were going to do it and monitored your progress along the way. As a result you will have ended up achieving your ambition and feel totally great about doing so.

## Time to act

Whatever your ambitions are, if you want to achieve them, you need to get yourself organised and commit the time and effort to doing so. No-one is going to do this for you and it is purely down to your own motivation. The rewards are, however, significant.

Even as you start to think about these ambitions they can make your adrenaline start to flow and make the pulse quicken because they are something new, something exciting and challenging and will make your life more interesting and fulfilling. What a great way to spend your time rather than sitting contemplating getting older and discussing your list of ailments with anybody who is prepared to listen.

Achieving an ambition can create a tremendous feeling of well-being and a boost to your own self-esteem, making you feel a more valuable and knowledgeable person. This is a tremendous feeling to have at any time in your life but can be particularly valuable at an age when you may be more aware of your own limitations compared to your younger days.

There are also the memories you create by achieving your ambitions which will stay with you for the rest of your life. You may also have photographs or other materials that will also provide you with a physical reminder of your achievements.

Perhaps, however, the most important aspect of trying to achieve your ambitions is that you have tried. To look back on your life and wonder what those experiences would have been like, if you never even tried achieve them, is going to be frustrating and leave you with a feeling of being unfulfilled. Nobody wants to end up with thoughts of 'if only' so make sure that you do not leave it too late.

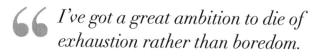 *I've got a great ambition to die of exhaustion rather than boredom.*

Thomas Carlyle

---

## MEMORY JOGGERS

◎ Consider if your life is too busy for achieving ambitions.
◎ Your life is not pre-scripted and you can choose what you want to do.
◎ It is better to have tried to achieve something and failed than never to have tried at all.
◎ Start taking practical steps to achieving ambitions by planning what you are going to do.
◎ Prioritise your list of ambitions before you start.

◎ Your ambitions may be challenging but make them enjoyable too.

◎ What are you waiting for?…Now is the time to get started!

# 9.

## MONEY MATTERS

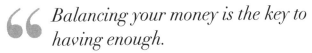 *Balancing your money is the key to having enough.*

Elizabeth Warren

### Why it matters

They say that money cannot buy you happiness and that may well be true but it certainly has the potential to make life a whole lot easier and considerably more enjoyable by opening doors to places that will make you smile. At a practical level it will also make sure that you can pay all those ever-rising bills and hopefully leave a bit over to occasionally treat yourself.

Whether you are actually sixty, or fall just either side of that age, it is a time in life when, more than ever, you need to be aware of your finances and know what resources you have available to you by way of both capital and income.

Everybody's financial circumstances will be different and you need to have a good idea of what yours are because, to state it simply, nobody else is going to take that responsibility for you.

You may be in the very fortunate position to have sufficient capital and on-going income to feel secure for the rest of your life. If that is the case for you then you are well placed and should be pleased with yourself that you have managed to put yourself in that position. Alternatively you may find yourself in the difficult position of having little or no capital and having to survive on a small income. This can be an extremely uncomfortable and worrying position, in which to find yourself.

Many people at this age will, more than likely, fall in between these two positions with some capital saved up and a reliable and on-going source of income from pensions and investments. Some will have capital but this will be tied up in the value of their home so it is unlikely to be a liquid asset, from which to derive any extra income.

## Changing financial circumstances

In recent years the financial situation for people retiring has changed significantly because of a combination of several factors.

For a start, the increase in life expectancy has put enormous financial pressure on corporate pension funds as well as state-funded pensions. This has been further worsened by the economic climate which prevailed on a global scale in the early twenty-first century. These difficult years reduced company earnings and hampered their ability to meet the demands of their own pension funds. The funds themselves also suffered significantly from poor stock market returns and low interest rates. Low investment returns naturally resulted in less money being available to distribute to pensioners.

As a result of these prevailing factors many companies abandoned final salary pension schemes in favour of personal pensions. The ultimate pension benefits from these schemes, for the individual concerned, will depend upon the level of contributions made rather than their final salary and, as a result, are likely to be less generous.

For state-funded pensions, governments have resorted to extending retirement ages so that you have to wait longer before you start receiving your pension. This can mean that you either have to work longer to maintain your income or survive on a lesser income for longer than expected.

If you were fortunate enough to have saved some cash for your retirement the prevailing low interest rates have meant that returns have been very poor. As a result you may have had to use some of your capital to meet your outgoings as living costs continued to rise.

Many companies listed on world stock markets have had to cut their dividend payments to shareholders because of weaker profits, so investors in equities and unit trusts have also experienced a fall in their returns. If you were unfortunate enough to be a shareholder in many of the banks you will have seen this source of dividend income decline as well as suffering a significant loss of capital.

With all these negative factors there has been little or no good news for those of us expecting to retire with a good pension and the situation is very unlikely to get any better in the future. This is particularly the result of life expectancy continuing to increase, brought about by medical advances and improvements in living standards, which in turn will mean that pensions and annuities will need even greater funding. Living longer is certainly a wonderfully big plus of modern life but it is not so good if you have to endure it in poverty.

## Managing your money

### Preparing your own budgets

You therefore need to ask yourself if you can you take sufficient responsibility for your own finances?

Can you make sure that your life is as comfortable as possible and free of the worry of having insufficient income? You will also want to know if you have sufficient resources to allow you to indulge in the odd treat as well as pursuing any of your ambitions.

The starting point to do this is to prepare your own budget and financial status check. That may sound fairly onerous for someone who has not had too much dealing with finances or figures before, but in reality it is fairly straightforward.

The starting point is to prepare a budget, or simple forecast, of your income and your outgoings (what you anticipate spending). This is best done initially for one calendar year in advance as this will give you a full picture of what you can expect to happen each year whereas a shorter period may be misleading as it could exclude some annual income or bills.

### Forecast your expenditure

If you can use your computer to prepare a simple spread sheet then do so, but if spread sheets are not your forte, it is just as easy to use a piece of A4 paper. Start by putting horizontally along the top of the page the twelve months of the year, starting with January and ending with December, and add a Total column at the end.

Vertically, down the left hand side of the page, enter the description of the types of payments you know you have to make. This would be items like mortgage or rent; council tax; electricity and gas; water charges; insurances; telephone; food; petrol; clothing and whatever else on which you regularly spend money. A good way to identify all these areas of expenditure is to go through your bank statements and monthly credit card bills. These will give you a good indication of the regular payments you make and the types of expenses you have.

To avoid an endless list you might just want to have a final category of miscellaneous payments which will deal, in one total, with all the small payments you make each month. At the end of your expenditure list put a Total heading for the total monthly expenditure and the overall total for the year.

The next step is to then enter in the column, under each month, how much you spend on each item you have listed. Some will be quite simple to do as you will be paying the same amount each month, possibly by direct debit, such as for your rent or mortgage. Some payments may not be every month but fall quarterly or annually such as for telephone or insurances. For these simply enter the amount you expect to pay in the column for the relevant month. Checking what you have paid in the past will help you estimate these costs in the future. In your miscellaneous section enter a total sum you spend each month which is not detailed under any of the other headings. You may need to estimate this and put a round sum such as £100 or £200 per month depending on what you think you spend.

Within this miscellaneous sum you would include all the bits and pieces you pay out every month for such things as a cup of coffee when out shopping or buying a newspaper or magazine. You do not want to list all these things individually as to do so will probably mean that you run out of paper!

Once you are pretty much satisfied that you have listed all the individual sums of money that you anticipate you will spend each month, your next step is to add up each monthly column so that you can see what your total outgoings will be for each month. Once you have done this for each month you can add all the monthly totals together to give you a final total of your spending budget for the year ahead.

By now you should have a fairly clear and accurate picture of what you will be spending in the next twelve months. You will also be able to see the amount for each month which will indicate the months in which you might need to find a bit extra to meet all of your outgoings. This may be the case at such times as holidays or Christmas when you know that you will be spending a little more than normal.

### Forecast your income

The next step in preparing your budget is to use a separate sheet of paper to work out your budgeted income for the year ahead.

Once again list the months across the top of the page and a

total column at the end then list down the left hand side of the page the headings for each source of income you have.

These will depend on your current situation but could involve a wage or salary; personal pension; state pension; benefits; interest on savings; other investment income or any other source of income you have.

Now enter in each column the amount you expect to receive each month from each source of income. Some income may be the same each month and some may vary both in amount and frequency so you will just have to be aware of these differences as you prepare your lists. Once again your previous bank or building society statements will help you find a lot of this information.

Once you have finished listing your income for each month you will need to add up each monthly column to show you how much income in total you can expect each month. Then add together all the monthly totals to give your total income for the year and write this amount in the total column.

Now you are really starting to get somewhere in getting to grips with your finances. The two budgets you have prepared will give you a clear indication of how much income you can expect in each month in the year ahead and what your spending will be.

### Summarise your expenditure and income

Now you need to prepare a third sheet of paper to summarise your finances. Once again list the twelve months of the year ahead across the top of the page and once again finish with a total column.

On the left hand side of your page you need to list, down the page, three headings which will be Outgoings, Income and Difference.

Next to the Outgoings heading enter, across the page in each month, the total amount you have calculated in your budget that you expect to spend each month. Next to the Income heading list, across the page, month by month, the total amount you have calculated you will receive in each of those months.

Next to the Difference heading you simply need to work out for each month, the difference between your total outgoings and your total income. This will show you that you either have more income in a month than you have outgoings (a surplus) or conversely that you have more outgoings budgeted in a month than you have income (a deficit).

One final calculation to do is to add up all the monthly surpluses and then take away all the monthly deficits to see what your overall situation is for the year. This final total will indicate if, for the whole year, you have enough income to pay for all you outgoings. If you have, your total will be a positive surplus but if not the total will be a negative deficit.

## Understanding your financial position

With all of this information you will now have an excellent starting point to control your finances. You will probably also find that in preparing this information you have gained a much more detailed understanding of your finances which has already put you in a much stronger position to take any action that may be necessary.

If your budgets have revealed that your expected income is more than enough to cope with budgeted outgoings, then congratulations, you are in a good and healthy financial position. With the surplus income you anticipate having you may want to plan to save some or instead you may wish to treat yourself to some luxury that takes your fancy.

### Take care! Mistakes can happen

A word of caution is advisable here, because if you are new to budgeting you should be careful that you have not forgotten any items of expenditure. It is easily done and you should be aware that unexpected bills can always crop up and spoil even the best of plans.

If you think that you are better off than you really are, and spend the money you think you have to spare, you could put yourself in a difficult position if an unexpected bill suddenly crops up.

If your budgets have revealed that your expected income over the next year is not going to be sufficient to meet your outgoings you are now in a better position to take action, and try to correct this. This is obviously a worrying problem that you have to face up to. One thing is for sure; simply ignoring the problem will not make it go away. It is much better to have control of the situation so that you can start planning what to do before you end up in debt.

## Dealing with a shortfall in your finances

The first thing you must do is to look at all the items, on which you plan to spend money, to see if you can make any cut-backs or savings. Obviously some costs will be difficult to do much about particularly when it comes to items like rents, mortgages and utility costs. Other costs may be easier to reduce so it really is a case of just identifying what your real needs are and what you can do without or can cut back on.

Other ways to cut costs may involve shopping around more for utility providers; looking for the cheapest sources for loans and mortgages and generally reducing bills by using less of whatever you are paying for. It is true that every little helps.

If you have reached a point where you have reduced your outgoings as much as you can and you still find that your income simply is not sufficient to match your needs you need to take even further action.

Running up debts and borrowing money will ultimately only end in more problems.

An alternative is that you could start to consider ways in which you might increase your income. If you are not working you could try to get a part time job to generate a little extra cash. To continue working even past normal retirement age is becoming increasingly popular not only for the extra cash but also to keep active. Older employees are often favoured by businesses because they are considered to be more reliable, honest and loyal.

If you cannot find any suitable part time work you might consider working from home and setting up your own small business. Many people have skills which they have acquired throughout their lifetime, for which others would gladly pay. Working for yourself also has the benefit of more flexible working hours.

It is really down to 'needs must' as you will have to decide for yourself how you can deal with your forecasted excess of spending over income. One thing is for sure, if you ignore it you will eventually end up with a serious problem whereas sound planning, by way of budgeting, and corrective action will likely avoid such a situation arising.

## Understanding your capital resources

In taking full control of your finances you will also need to have a clear understanding of what capital you may have. This could be bank or building society savings, stock market investments, unit trusts, or even cash stashed under the bed!

These capital assets are relatively liquid and can be used not only to provide extra income but also to plug any shortfalls in your budget so you need to ensure that you know what you have and how you can go about using them when you need to.

You may also need them to fund significant capital outgoings that are not included in your monthly budget. For example, the purchase of a new car or a special anniversary holiday are one-offs that can be met out of your capital.

You also need to monitor closely the investment performance of these types of asset and ensure that you are maximising your income from them and also not taking undue risks with your capital. If, for example, you have money in a bank or building society you need to check frequently that you are getting the best rate of interest available. Rates change all the time and you need to keep up to date with them to ensure that you do not miss out. This task has been made relatively easy nowadays thanks to the internet.

Some investments will also be riskier than others and you need to ensure that your capital is safe. If you invest in stocks and shares these can be extremely volatile and should only be considered by the brave hearted and you should ensure that the sums you invest are not essential to your financial well-being in the future.

If you have saved into a pension fund that you can use to provide a pension in retirement you will need to exercise care if you decide to purchase an annuity. Although new pension rules in the UK mean that you no longer have to purchase an annuity many people will still feel that this is the best way to provide an ongoing income for the rest of their life. The best practise for this is to shop around with annuity providers to understand who is going to be the best for you. This may not be the pension company, with which you have accumulated your funds. If you are uncertain how to go about this you may wish to speak with a qualified financial advisor who will give you impartial advice on this matter. There will be some fees involved in doing so.

The new pension rules in the UK mean that you will be able to access much more quickly the funds you have saved into your pension pot. This may sound tempting but you should be very cautious about doing so. The statistics showing life expectancy indicate that we can expect to live longer than ever before. Whilst that is good news, the downside will be that you will need more money to fund your retirement. Extensively dipping into your pension fund too quickly may cause you considerable financial hardship as you get older. Again, it may be wise to seek the advice of a qualified financial advisor before taking any action.

You may also have other capital assets such as a property, antiques or jewellery which, while valuable, are less liquid and therefore if at any time you need to release cash from them, will need to be carefully planned in advance. If you are unprepared financially and have to quickly realise these less liquid assets you are invariably likely to find that you get less than they are worth.

## Keeping up to date with your finances

The process of budgeting and understanding your finances is absolutely key to exercising control over your financial affairs and to avoiding nasty surprises in the future. As such, it should not just be a one off exercise as it needs updating regularly as circumstances will change over time.

A good way to keep this under control is to regularly review how much your income and expenditure has been each month in comparison to the budget you prepared. This will soon make it clear to you whether or not you have made some omissions and are paying out more than you thought. Equally it may indicate that you have over budgeted your expenses or under estimated your income and things are not as bad as you thought!

Another key element of doing this exercise is that it will soon indicate if you are paying out things that you should no longer be paying, such as direct debits that you have forgotten to cancel. It may also surprise you, in an unwelcome way, just how much you are spending on non-necessities such as clothes or eating out. Even if you can afford them it may cause you to stop and think if you really should be spending your money in that way.

The more that you are able to plan and review your finances, the greater degree of control you have over them. Not only will this stop you getting in a mess with your finances but will be a great deal less stressful for you so that your time and energy can be spent in Making The Most Of *It*.

## Searching for a solution to financial problems

The big question remains for those who have reached this age and, having done their budgets, have come to the conclusion that they simply do not have enough money.

Once you have gone through your budgets and, saved all the money you can, you may still be in the unpleasant and worrying situation where your outgoings exceed your income.

This is a very difficult situation but the solution still does not rest in borrowing money or running up debts. With insufficient income to repay borrowed sums you will eventually end up in a worse position. Debt will pile upon debt until it all becomes totally unmanageable. You must look hard to see how you can get outside help without resorting to borrowing. As accountants often say:

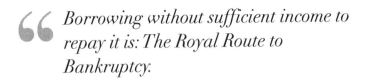

> *Borrowing without sufficient income to repay it is: The Royal Route to Bankruptcy.*

You may, for example, be entitled to social security benefits because of your circumstances and you should explore this avenue even though you may have never needed to previously. This is what the benefit system exists for; to help those who genuinely cannot support themselves.

There also exist many charitable bodies that will give support and help with much needed resources to those in need. Sometimes pride stands in the way of asking for help but this should not prevent you from doing so. Remember the old adage that 'Pride comes before a fall'.

Try hard to use your own abilities and resources to find ways to generate extra cash for yourself even if you cannot find part time work or do not have a business idea. For example, a further potential source of income is trading on eBay or at car boot sales. Many find these not only lucrative sources of income but also provide an enjoyable way of spending their time.

Sometimes the hardest thing is to accept that you have to do something different, to what you would normally do, to make ends meet. Stepping out of your comfort zone can be extremely unnerving. Once you do it however, you may be surprised just how much you enjoy it and what a welcome difference it makes to your finances.

Money may not buy you happiness but by ensuring that you have sufficient to meet your needs, with perhaps a little bit over to Make The Most Of *It*, you will find that life is less stressful and certainly more enjoyable.

Money matters because we all need it to pay for the necessities of life and to avoid struggling with our finances. Taking responsibility for you financial well-being is absolutely essential even though you may not enjoy doing so.

Do not leave it too late!

 *Too many people spend money they don't have, to buy things they don't want, to impress people they don't like.*

Will Smith

---

## MEMORY JOGGERS

- ◎ Good control over your finances brings peace of mind and makes life more enjoyable.
- ◎ Being constantly overspent creates stress and worry.
- ◎ Pensions are changing fast and are not as safe as they used to be.
- ◎ Time to control your finances by preparing a budget.
- ◎ Use your budget to really understand your finances.
- ◎ If your budget reveals a shortfall in your finances, now is the time to act.
- ◎ Borrowing money to cover your shortfall is not a permanent answer.

◎ Understand all your financial assets and how they are invested.

◎ Review your finances regularly and keep on top of them.

# 10.

## WHAT CAN HOLD YOU BACK FROM MAKING THE MOST OF *IT*!

### Are you ready for change?

 *Change will not come if we wait for some other person, or if we wait for some other time. We are the ones we've been waiting for. We are the change that we seek.*

Barack Obama

When reading this book you will have gradually realised that you will need to be making a lot of plans and setting yourself many challenging goals to ensure that you are really fulfilling your life from sixty onwards.

For you to achieve all of your plans and goals it is likely to involve major change in your life and your established routine. You may feel really excited at the prospect of these changes and the differences they will make to your life. Others may feel slightly concerned and uneasy about them.

Many of the practical steps involved in making these changes have already been explained in the earlier chapters but there are also important psychological aspects to change which should be considered.

To allow your mind to freely accept the changes that your goals and challenges require, your thinking will need to be flexible, non-extreme and totally rational. You will need to be able to put up with frustration when things go wrong; remember that whatever your situation, things could be worse – and be tolerant of yourself and others as you set out to achieve your goals. They will be worth it.

Experiencing setbacks along the way does not mean that you have got it wrong or that your plans are not achievable. You will need perseverance and faith in yourself as you set about fulfilling your objectives. The ultimate rewards will make your life so much more interesting and rewarding.

Two important psychological considerations you should be aware of are how to cope with regrets from your earlier life and the creeping paralysis of procrastination or the 'Thief of Time.' Both of these can be looked upon as psychological blocks and you will need to know how to recognise them and, importantly, how to overcome them should they slow you down in your pursuit of Making The Most Of It.

## Dealing with regrets

By the time you have lived sixty years you will have made a lot of decisions and choices during your life. These will be lodged in your memory and from time to time will surface as an emotion and affect the way you feel. These may be good and happy emotions and you will welcome them. Some things that have happened in the past may alternatively cause emotions such as disappointment or sadness.

The good and positive memories you have are worth dwelling on, from time to time, and sharing with others as they can make you feel good as you recall those happy events. They can bring a smile to your face on a cold winters' day or when things are not going quite so well.

However, there may be things we have done, or even not done, along the way, which we have later come to realise were not necessarily the best course of action for us. In later life they can frequently cause us to experience feelings such as sadness, dissatisfaction and even anger. They can also create in us a state of paralysis when it comes to trying something new or different as we may fear making another mistake.

Regrets can make us think about, and dwell on, what we might have done differently. The result is that in our later years when we should be Making The Most Of *It* we are instead spending time dealing with the past and not the here and now, let alone our very important futures.

Worrying about what happened in the past is a very unhealthy state of affairs for us. Importantly it is also a considerable waste of valuable time as our energies should be directed towards fulfilling ourselves over the rest of our lives and not mulling over and worrying about what might have been.

Yesterday has been and gone and however hard we try we cannot change what has been.

## Why do we have regrets?

Do we all have them?

Some people are often very hesitant about admitting to having regrets and even less inclined to discuss them. We should not be surprised at this as they are very private and personal thoughts and in acknowledging them we are admitting to mistakes in our past life. Few of us like admitting we were wrong. Having regrets can not only make us feel sad and dissatisfied but can also make us feel very vulnerable.

As we go through our lives though, we frequently have to make decisions that will change our lives. When doing so the fear of ultimately getting things wrong and having regrets is a powerful motivator. So much so that the fear can result in paralysis of the mind and, as a result, the decision is avoided.

Think back on your own life about choices you had to make about such subjects as your career; your relationships; your family; your home; your education; your finances and many more.

Some of these examples may be relevant to you:

◎ The hobby you never pursued which could have become a career but you opted for the safe choice instead.

◎ The boyfriend or girlfriend you stopped seeing and then never stopped thinking about.

◎ The hard earned money you invested without really checking first what you were getting into.

◎ The missed chance of pursuing your education through University or College and achieving better qualifications.

◎ Getting married too young and not experiencing more that life had to offer.

◎ Not taking the chance to travel when you had the opportunity.

We have all made decisions in the past and to act accordingly, often thinking to ourselves, 'I hope that I never regret this'.

We could only have made those choices on the facts we knew at the time, and the prevailing circumstances, and we hoped at that time we made the best choice. Sometimes, however, it turned out that we were wrong. Hindsight is a wonderful thing and makes it all so obvious and neither are we clairvoyants, with the ability to see into the future. Regrettably it can turn out that sometimes we made the wrong choice.

Now some people may say that they have no regrets at all and if that is the case then they have either been very clever along the way or very fortunate. As long as they believe that, it does not matter whether they actually made any bad choices or not, because they are not letting them affect how they are functioning in the here and now. No wasting time dwelling on the past for them, they are totally free to Make The Most Of It.

## Admitting our regrets

For many of us, however, there will be lurking in our minds these regrets about things we have done or maybe could have done differently. There maybe even sadness about things that we never quite got around to doing. Every time we think about them they raise some of those unpleasant and negative emotions within us that can only dampen the way we feel.

You may recognise that you have regrets and these are possibly being accentuated by the fact that ever advancing age is preventing you from changing what has happened. Very frustrating, annoying and anger provoking but now is the time to let go of those very negative feelings. It is time to stop letting them interfere with how you should be enjoying life now.

Now is the time to stop saying to yourself, 'If Only' because the simple truth is that you cannot change what has happened. The sorrow aroused in you is caused by past events and circumstances which are now beyond your control or your power to repair.

### *Do not waste time looking backwards unless you are planning to go that way*

Perhaps an easier way to look at how you are dealing with your regrets about the past is to compare your feelings with travelling on a train, on which you are sitting looking backwards as the train, and your life, speed forward. You can simply change the way you are viewing things by getting up and swapping seats so that you are now looking forward and have a clear view of where you are going.

There is a need to adopt a different approach if you are burdened with regrets. However, it is rather like telling somebody to calm down or get a grip when what they really need is help to relieve the problem that made them feel like that in the first place. We know that words are often cheap whereas practical help is often harder to get.

What is certain is that there are things you can be doing to prevent yourself moping about. You need to stop feeling sorry for yourself and letting your regrets shroud you in hopelessness and self-pity, paralysing you into inactivity. This is the time in your life when you should be super active in fulfilling your dreams with nothing holding you back.

### Steps to help you overcome your regrets

The first thing you need to do is identify exactly what the regret is that is troubling you. Is it the fact that you acted unwisely or did not act at all? Or is your regret more about the consequences or what might have been? Try and think this through and clarify it in your mind as it is important to understand exactly what is troubling you.

Next consider if what happened was brought about by circumstances beyond your control. In other words you could not have changed what happened even if you had wanted to. If this is the case, what is the point in even thinking of blaming yourself?

Allow yourself to recognise that everyone makes mistakes and it is not just you. Making mistakes is a major part of the way we learn and can make us better and stronger individuals. To make a mistake is very human and helps us to learn from it making us different from everyone else and in creating the person we have become.

Take time to recognise what you have subsequently learned from what happened and how it has since shaped your life for the better. This is an on-going process that will continue to benefit you for the rest of your life. The benefits that this bad experience has subsequently brought you can go a long way to off-setting the negativity of your regret.

List all the things in your life that you really are grateful for having or for experiencing. Not just possessions, but also relationships and good experiences in all the different aspects of your life both past and present. Weigh these up against the regrets and realise which way the scales tip. Many of us have so much to be grateful for and so much happiness in our lives so why are we troubling our minds with regrets?

Learn to live your life fully in the here and now and let the past be. If you think or talk about the past concentrate only on the good memories.

Keep moving forward and look with positive anticipation to discovering everything each new day brings you. Your life is like a book and you need to keep turning the pages to see what happens next. There is no point in continuously flicking back through the pages as nothing will be different from the first time you read it.

With this advice in mind take time to consider how *you* are going to stop worrying about *your* regrets and then deal with them. No-one wants to reach the end of their life and when asked to describe it can only say,

### Should have, might have, could have!
Stop swimming against the tide and move forward instead. You will find it a lot easier and a whole lot more enjoyable. This is a really important factor in gaining maximum fulfilment from the rest of your life in a positive manner. It may even inspire

you to get on and do something that you have always regretted not doing.

What a bonus that would be!

As always, Making The Most Of *It* depends on how determined each of us is to do exactly that and dwelling in the past with regrets is definitely not part of the plan.

## Procrastination and pottering

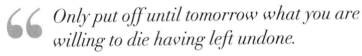 *Only put off until tomorrow what you are willing to die having left undone.*

Pablo Picasso

Probably the biggest danger you face to enjoying the rest of your life is the time you can waste in procrastination and pottering.

This may come as something of a surprise to you because, in all likelihood, it is not something that you have even stopped and thought about. Yet, just pause and consider for a moment (or procrastinate if you like) about how today, or maybe in the past few days, you have put off doing something you needed to do and have found yourself busy doing something else instead.

This is not to say you are doing nothing or are lazing about. Far from it, you are still busy, but instead of doing something that will really help make your life more fulfilling you are engaged in doing mundane and routine chores which could be done at any time. In other words you are pottering about (Cutting the grass? Reading the paper? Making another cup of coffee?)

So why does this happen? Why do we put off until tomorrow what could easily be done today? On a longer term basis why do we put off making beneficial changes in our lives instead of getting on with those changes and reaping the benefits?

There are reasons why we are prone to procrastinate, and as you read about them, you may identify one or more which cause you personally to put things off. If you recognise any, it would be useful for you to take time to write them down so that you can refer back to them later. Understanding the factors that cause you to waste time and behave in this way will help you to tackle them.

## Reasons we procrastinate
### *Seeking perfection*
Some people need to achieve perfection in everything they do. If you believe you are in this category you will know that you sometimes hold back from acting because you are concerned that the end result will be less than perfect in your eyes. For the outcome of your actions to be less than perfect can only be classed as a failure in your eyes and thus you delay and put off doing it.

If you are making plans to Make The Most Of *It*, you may never get around to implementing those plans because of fear. The fear of failure is the root cause of your procrastination. Just imagine embarking on learning a foreign language that is new to you. You really want to do it but in the back of your mind exists the fear that you will not be able to and you will end up failing. This is just too much to even contemplate so it is a lot easier simply avoiding getting started.

### Worrying too much

You may be a worrier and fear things going wrong so your mind becomes filled with 'what if' questions. You have made your plans to make sure that the rest of your life is fulfilling but you keep putting off implementing them because you are worried that something will go wrong. The thought alone of what may go wrong is quite overwhelming for you.

Thus you never go on that trip you really wanted to make because you are worried that you might not like it or may not be able to cope with it.

You never join that club, or tried that hobby that you fancied, because you are worried about making a fool of yourself. You end up avoiding doing things and just talk about them instead and eventually it is too late to do anything other than dream about your plans.

### Not liking being told what to do

Making The Most Of It may sometimes involve doing things that your partner wants to do. For some, this is difficult to accept because you just cannot bear to be told what to do by someone else – and definitely not by your partner.

They may be drawing up plans that involve the willing participation of the two of you but, because you are being told what to do, you make sure that you find every reason under the sun to avoid doing it.

It is not just down to whether you want to be involved or not, you procrastinate simply because it is not your idea in the first place. This basically boils down to a control issue as you are the type of person who always wants to do, what you want to do. You are likely only to pursue plans if they were your idea.

When this is the case you can end up not only failing to do what your partner wanted to do but potentially cause a serious rift with them as well.

You may ultimately think that it would have been easier, and more fulfilling, to be more cooperative in the first instance.

### Making too many plans

Some people can be prone to over organising and end up with too many plans and ambitions in their quest to make their life more fulfilling.

This can often end with many of their plans never getting started, let alone achieved and this can cause considerable frustration and disappointment.

For example, if Making The Most Of *It* for you involves studying and learning new skills, you may try to take on too many challenges at a time and instead of enjoying what you are doing you never get around to starting any of them properly. Priority is the key here otherwise it all just becomes a terrible muddle where nothing is achieved.

### The 'last minute' person

Of course, there is also the classic procrastination case of the ''last minute'' person.

146

You may be one yourself, or if not, you have probably come across someone that falls into this category. This is the person who will always leave everything until the last possible moment and as a result things frequently do not get done or it necessitates a change in plan. This is a lifetime habit for some people that is difficult to overcome.

Recognising that you behave like this is the first step in changing this habit.

## The cause of procrastination

So why does this happen? Why do we so easily fall into the trap of putting off until tomorrow what we should be cracking on and doing right now?

It is because procrastination is an emotional problem that exists within the affected individual and is a form of avoidance behaviour. Although none of us likes to own up to having an emotional problem it is something that needs to be faced if you find yourself procrastinating. Do you want to spend the rest of your life doing things that will enhance your enjoyment of life or would you rather just spend your time thinking about them?

To miss the opportunity to not make the most of whatever time you have left is indeed a serious act of folly on anyone's behalf.

## Overcoming procrastination

If, by now, you have become aware that procrastination is an issue for you, the good news is that you will have already taken the first step in dealing with it.

Recognising that you are putting off doing things, or at least, delaying getting on with them, requires a conscious act on your behalf. It also requires some mental strength to admit to yourself that your inaction is not doing you any favours and that you are, indeed, literally wasting your valuable time.

There is no need to feel ashamed of admitting that you are not getting on with things like you know you should. It is a common fault and affects most of us from time to time. The important fact is that you are aware of it and are now prepared to do something about it.

So what should you do next, once you have realised that you are not getting on with your lifetime plans like you really want to?

It is quite simple, you should make a list of all the things that you want to do and then you must work through that list in order of priority until you have done everything. In other words, you change your behaviour as it is all about action rather than struggling with feelings and emotions. Stop thinking about doing it and start actually getting on with it, however uncomfortable you may initially find this makes you feel.

Once you start you will likely experience an overwhelming sense of relief at taking positive action that will in turn create a feel-good factor for you. Just getting on with your plans to Make The Most Of *It* will likely give you a tremendous feeling of pleasure and a good start to being fulfilled. This is a welcome and motivating taste of the long-term gains that your action is going to bring you rather than the feeling of frustration that procrastination and inactivity are bound to breed.

Once you start the ball rolling, and turn inactivity into action, it is important that you stay focussed and ensure that the plans or goals that you are working on are fully pursued. You do not want to allow complacency to creep back in and open the door to further delays caused by your old enemy, procrastination.

Persistence is the key, as it is all too easy to let enthusiasm dwindle, particularly if your progress in achieving your goals is not initially as smooth as you would like. To be persistent you need willpower and if you find that you are somewhat short of that attribute consider this for a moment and say to yourself; 'Nobody is going to fulfil my life for me and if I miss the chance to live my life to the full then I only have myself to blame.'

 *You may delay but time will not.*
Benjamin Franklin

Act now before time passes you by. Make The Most Of *It!*

---

### MEMORY JOGGERS

---

◎ Change is not easy; you need mental strength, perseverance and willpower.
◎ Dwelling on regrets from the past can paralyse us into inactivity in the present.
◎ If you continue looking backwards you will probably end up going that way.

◎ Take time to specifically deal with regrets once and for all.

◎ It is always easy to put off until tomorrow what can be done today.

◎ Time wasted is never regained – use it or lose it!

# 11.

## MINDFULNESS

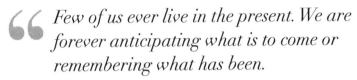

> *Few of us ever live in the present. We are forever anticipating what is to come or remembering what has been.*
>
> Louis L'Amour

### Free your mind to Make The Most Of It

You have probably noticed that the days and weeks seem to pass by so quickly. Suddenly you find that another year has slipped by. It seems that the older we get the quicker the time goes. If only we could slow it down and have the time to appreciate more of the world around us.

For those, who at sixty, have already retired from work you will know that the first question everybody asks you when you tell them that you are retired is, 'What do you do with your time?'

It is likely that you will reply that you are so busy that you just have no idea how you ever had time to go to work.

The simple fact is that we live in a world where there is so much to occupy us and fill our minds that we have little time left over simply to enjoy relaxing. Our minds seem to be constantly occupied with what we are doing and what we need to do next.

It is not that the clock now moves faster than when you were young; it is, instead, that your thoughts are constantly occupied and time seems to pass more quickly as a result.

## What makes our time pass so quickly?

Why are we so preoccupied that we have so little time simply to relax and appreciate the wonders of the world around us?

To understand what has happened we need to give some consideration to how our lives have changed in recent years.

There is no doubt that since the middle of the twentieth century the world has changed at an amazing pace. As time progresses the speed of change continues to accelerate at a frantic, non-stop pace, and our lifestyles have changed accordingly.

### *Technology*

A major contributor to the changes in our lives is technology and the huge difference this had made to communications. We now have a constant bombardment of messages and information coming at us from numerous sources. Whether it is our mobile phones, pads or computers, television or radio, the information comes at us constantly and is available twenty-four hours every day.

Communication with the furthest parts of the world is simple and cost effective and whatever your need to communicate or be communicated with, it can happen in seconds.

We can shop online non-stop, we can study online at any hour of any day, we can book our holidays and make our travel arrangements in the middle of the night, and manage our finances online at any hour on any day. We can watch television at any time, access our favourite music and listen to the latest news at any time and in any place.

With access to all this information online and the availability to service all our needs constantly we have come to accept that our lives should be lived in this instant way.

Technology has done many wonderful things for our world but it has also become a major part of our lives and occupies so much of our time.

### Cheap and easy travel

A further change to the way we live is the revolution that has taken place in travelling. We now take for granted that we are able to journey quickly and cheaply to destinations in a manner that, a few years ago, would have seemed impossible.

It is common nowadays to fly hundreds of miles just for a weekend break, let alone a holiday, because it is so easy to do and relatively inexpensive. As a result our expectations surrounding travel have totally changed and the world has become a much smaller place. Naturally we want to take advantage of the opportunity to see all those wondrous sights.

Instead of relaxing and enjoying our homes we are tempted to take off for a break when we have a spare few days spending our time constantly on the go rather than enjoying our own surroundings.

## Social changes

There has also been another important change in the way we lead our lives that has had a major impact on how we spend our time. This relates to the social changes which have occurred in the relationship between men and women. The post Second World War baby-boom created an expectation that the man would go to work and earn income to provide for his family, while the woman would stay at home to do the housework and look after the children.

This situation has gradually disappeared as both parties either want to work or need financially to have two incomes to support their lifestyle. This creates time pressures as, after a hard day at work, there will still be the domestic chores, with which to deal. Someone has to take on the cooking of meals, the washing and ironing, the cleaning and gardening and the endless chores which still need to be done.

## Busy lives; little time to relax

As a result there is precious little time to relax and unwind. The body and mind are constantly on the go, moving rapidly from one task to another or from one thought to the next. As we do one thing our minds are often in a different place focussing on something that has happened during the day or on events that are to happen in the future. Our physical actions go on auto pilot as our minds and emotions wander off in numerous directions. Sometimes these thoughts are useful to us and may be pleasant but often they can be stress provoking making us feel upset and worried. We find that lack of time means that we are struggling to cope with everything we know needs doing. Our minds become overloaded and stressed.

Often negative thoughts can simply barge into our minds, unwanted and unhelpful and as they do so, they provoke the stressful emotions that can affect our physical and emotional well-being.

Throughout our lives we are conditioning our bodies and minds to accept that we should be constantly busy and as a result we can often experience a feeling of guilt if we slow down for a while and do nothing. Our minds soon become occupied with jobs to do, problems to deal with and arrangements to make.

By the time we reach sixty we have become well and truly busy people with our minds constantly occupied with thoughts of what we will be doing next.

We may still be working, we may be helping to look after the grandchildren, we may even be trying to Make The Most Of It and making plans to enjoy ourselves. Life remains hectic and challenging with little time to spare.

The problem with failing to take time out, time to relax the body and the mind, is that we are perpetuating a lifestyle that is not only making time pass in a blur but which may also cause harm to our physical and emotional health.

Having survived what may have been a hectic and potentially unhealthy lifestyle for sixty years, do you still want to perpetuate this behaviour?

## Time for a change?

We may want to have lots of things to do in our lives and be fulfilled but we also need to make sure that we remove stress from our lives and remain well.

After all, reaching sixty is only the start of the rest of our lives and our nature is to want to live to a ripe old age. If we are to do so, however, we also need to enjoy good physical and mental health. Without those we will be unable to lead a fulfilling life and be as active as we would want.

In order to enhance our well-being and resilience many people have turned to Mindfulness to help them achieve these objectives.

Mindfulness is simply being aware at any given time of our own physical sensations as well as our thoughts and feelings. In our minds we will constantly experience thoughts but by being intentionally alert to unhelpful thoughts and emotions we can stop ourselves being overwhelmed by them. If our thoughts are constantly occupied in dealing with regrets or fretting over events that have occurred, or are yet to happen, we are likely to feel stressed and emotionally distressed.

By engaging in Mindfulness we can identify those thoughts and calm our emotional responses. We are able to deal with the negative thoughts in a non-stressful manner.

## Experience the present moment

Mindfulness is very much about experiencing the present moment rather than letting our minds become dominated with thoughts of the past and concerns over the future. When we find ourselves dwelling on our past or worrying about the future we need, instead, to direct our minds to focus our awareness on where we are in the present and of being in the present moment.

In practising mindfulness there is a need to engage in living our lives on a daily basis, with a deliberate focus on the here and now and having an alert awareness of thoughts and events that may attempt to distract from this path. We need to be able to take notice and pay attention to the world around us and focus on the here and now.

In doing so we need to be able to experience the full sensory awareness of our current environment and be aware of our own physical, psychological and emotional responses to this environment.

For example as you travel to work, rather than being concerned about the meeting you are to have, you instead take note of the sensory experiences that the journey brings you. The things you see, their colours and shapes; the scents and smells you experience; the sounds that you hear and of which you are aware. Your thoughts are engaged in experiencing and exploring these aspects of your environment currently taking place and nothing else.

As you sit in a garden, instead of being concerned about something which is happening tomorrow, focus instead on feeling the warmth of the sun on your face; the smell of the flowers gently wafting on the breeze; the chirping of the birds. Let your mind not only experience these sensory pleasures but be aware of how relaxed your body feels and how your emotions are so positive.

Mindfulness is not initially an easy state to achieve. As we have seen, our minds and bodies have been trained throughout our lives to be in a high state of alert. Constantly doing, continuously thinking, analysing, worrying, and scheming. If you can recognise that you still live your life in this way then now would be a good time to stop and take stock of what you are doing. You want to Make The Most Of It, but to do so, you need to make sure that you have your life under your control.

You need to ensure that you are in control of your thoughts and emotions and that you are able to free your mind to live your life at your pace and in the way that you want. Making plans to fulfil your life is an integral part of Making The Most Of It, but you need to make sure that you are in a good physical and psychological state to do so.

If you still feel that there is more to life than you are currently experiencing, then there probably is! But you need to stop and take notice to ensure that it does not simply pass you by.

## Learning Mindfulness

You may be feeling that Mindfulness sounds like a good idea but are not sure that it is for you or that you have the time to experience it.

As with everything in life, if you never try it, you will never know if it works for you. The great thing about Mindfulness is that you can practice it at any time, in any location, in the amount of time that suits you.

Here are some of the ways you can try it for yourself:

Next time you are sitting, just focus your attention on how your body feels and on your breathing. Make sure that your breathing is slow and relaxed and take a few minutes to focus your thoughts on the sensations this creates within your body. Do this regularly throughout the day, as the opportunity presents itself, and you will find it wonderfully calming and that it will slow down time for you.

If you find yourself stuck in a traffic jam or waiting in a queue, instead of getting steamed up because of the delay, take the opportunity to study the physical world around you. Become aware of the clouds in the sky, the buildings or trees or whatever objects are in view. Take time to see them properly and allow your thoughts to temporarily dwell on what you see rather than become agitated with the wait. You will find that your emotions become calmer and you will feel less stressed. Enjoy the world around you rather than feel the anger.

Sitting in the doctor's waiting room and still waiting although your appointment was thirty minutes ago and definitely feeling stressed and becoming increasingly annoyed. These unpleasant and unwanted emotions are dominating your thoughts and not doing you any good as you continue to wait. Instead, take the time to once again focus on your breathing and ensure that it is slow and regular. Take the time to gaze around you and become totally aware of your surrounding environment. Make sure that you actually see what is around you by thinking about and understanding what you see.

Take a few minutes, whenever you can, to walk in your garden or in a park and do nothing but absorb yourself in your surroundings. Walk slowly and allow your body to relax as you listen to the sounds of nature; pay attention to the colour of the plants and flowers and breathe in the fresh tasting air. Have a full awareness of the present moment and shut out negative thoughts and concerns.

Mindfulness is simply a word to describe the ability to control your mind to bring you relaxation and a feeling of well-being that can often be in short supply in our lives. It slows you and the world around you down, making time seem to pass more slowly.

You may find it quite difficult initially to get your mind to be able to put aside your thoughts and to concentrate instead on the present moment. This is understandable as we have spent so much of our lives to date allowing our minds to be dominated by the past and the future. It has resulted in us living our lives on auto-pilot. The key is to persevere with Mindfulness and gradually you will find that you are able to exercise greater control over your thoughts. You will find yourself feeling calmer and less harassed as you live your life at a pace you enjoy.

Reaching sixty is a great opportunity to use Mindfulness to slow your life down to give you the freedom of thought and the benefit of time to enjoy yourself. Take control of your mind and help free yourself of the negative thoughts that are harmful to you.

If you want to be able to Make The Most Of *It* with no distractions holding you back, Mindfulness could be the answer for you.

*The present moment is filled with joy and happiness. If you are attentive you will see it.*

Thich Nhat Hanh

## MEMORY JOGGERS

◎ Time passes too quickly when we are preoccupied with thoughts about what has happened and what is coming next.

◎ Life has changed and leaves no time to relax the mind.

◎ Be alert to unhelpful thoughts and feelings when they fill your mind.

◎ Negative thoughts produce negative feelings creating stress and demotivating us.

◎ Focus on the here and now and learn to make your mind more aware of the present moment.

◎ Persevere with Mindfulness and your mind will gradually learn to control your thoughts.

◎ Practise mindfulness wherever you are and at any time and time will slow down.

# 12.

## MAKING THE MOST OF *IT* ! – TOP TEN TIPS

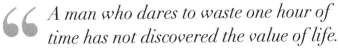

> *A man who dares to waste one hour of time has not discovered the value of life.*
>
> Charles Darwin

### 1. Exercise your body and mind regularly

Make sure that on a regular basis you are physically active and it will bring you many benefits. It can help you maintain a healthy weight and avoid illnesses associated with obesity. It strengthens the muscles and helps your energy levels. Physical exercise is also excellent for improving mental well-being and alertness. It may also help you to look fit and well which is great for your self-esteem. Try and achieve in the region of three hours of exercise every week.

### 2. You are what you eat... so eat well

Take care to ensure that your daily diet includes foods that have a high nutritional value. These are foods with nutrients such as vitamins, fibre and minerals and which have low contents of sugar and fat. Try not to eat much processed food. Good food is good for your weight, good for the way you look, good for your energy levels and good for you brain. It costs no more to eat healthy foods than it does unhealthy ones.

Why eat anything else?

## 3. Control your drinking and quit smoking

There are so many bad effects of smoking that it is amazing that so many people still do so. From a health perspective smoking can cause numerous chronic and life threatening illnesses that may either end your life prematurely or at least prevent you from enjoying it. Excessive consumption of alcohol is just as dangerous and can also cause chronic illnesses that are going to limit your lifestyle. It is quite easy to find out the advisable limits for drinking and to monitor how much you are consuming. Just enjoy it without abusing it.

## 4. Look after your health and have regular check-ups

The emphasis today is on preventing illness rather than curing it and this is why so many people are living longer and enjoying more active lifestyles. Go and see your doctor and get regular checks for your blood pressure. Have your blood tested for cholesterol levels and other indicators. This way, if anything is going wrong it can be detected at an early stage and treatment can be carried out to deal with it. It is no good staying away from your doctor and avoiding checks or not asking for help if you are aware that something is not quite right. Health problems rarely solve themselves but your doctor probably can offer a solution, so get yourself checked out.

## 5. Spend only what you can afford

Controlling your finances is paramount and you must ensure that you understand what your income and outgoings are going to be. Once you have done this you will be in a position to know if you can meet all of your financial commitments and not end up in debt. This way you will only spend what you can afford. You will also be aware if you are fortunate enough to have some money spare every month to allow you do the extra things you want to do without getting yourself into debt.

## 6. Make the most of family and friends

Life can potentially be quite lonely as we grow older, particularly once we leave work and retire. If you have family and friends however, you should make sure that you work at your relationships with them because if you ignore them they are likely to ignore you. Better to make an effort to foster these relationships and enjoy each other's company.

Make an effort to gain new friends and develop new relationships if you need to.

That's far better than being lonely.

## 7. Realise your ambitions

There is still plenty of time to do the things in life that you have always wanted, but there is no point in waiting. Once you have made up your mind and made your plans you need to get on with them. This is your chance to do the things that you always wanted, but never quite got around to. Avoid procrastination and self-doubt as these will just prevent you from enjoying yourself and being fulfilled.

Remember that if you miss out in this lifetime you will never get another opportunity.

## 8. Make a change and try something different

We can easily fall into the habit of doing the same things we have always done, a bit like going to the same place on holiday every year or always eating the same kind of food. Now is the chance to step outside your comfort zone and do something entirely different. Something that you never thought about doing before or maybe something that you never believed you could do. Experiencing something new is like a breath of fresh air and can stimulate your desire for more new experiences. It can boost your self esteem, activate your mind and bring new friendships.

## 9. Avoid living with regrets

There is no point in worrying about something you cannot change. It is in the past and nothing will ever change it. You need to look forward instead of backwards because what has gone has gone forever. If these negative thoughts do cross your mind from time to time just consider them as part of your learning curve and think instead of all the things that you have got right. Look upon life's experiences in a positive rather than negative way.

Turn the page and move on.

## 10. Don't act your age

If you think that you are old, behave like you are old, dress like you are old, look like you are old, then you are, undoubtedly, already old. You have made your choice and that is up to you. However, the age of sixty is no longer an old age. Life expectancy rates are increasing every year and attitudes to age are constantly changing. If you want to feel younger then act younger. It may be easier to be complacent about your age but if you really want to avoid looking old you can do something about it.

## In Conclusion – or it may be just the start for you

The ageing process is unfortunately not a perception, as some people would try to convince you, because it is most definitely a reality.

It is the way we deal with it which is the important point about growing older because there is no need to surrender to it and allow it only to be a negative process.

It is not the beginning of the end… it is a chance for a new beginning.

You owe it to yourself to do everything you can to maximise your life from sixty onwards and enjoy every moment of it by living a fulfilled, stress free life. The choice is yours.

You have a huge chunk of your life still ahead of you and you owe it to yourself to have some fun and Make The Most Of *It!*

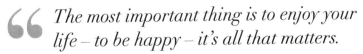

*The most important thing is to enjoy your life – to be happy – it's all that matters.*

Audrey Hepburn

167

# THE AUTHOR

Richard Jackson is a retired Fellow of The Institute of Chartered Accountants who now enjoys numerous pursuits and hobbies in an active retirement.

Amongst these pursuits are keeping fit; playing golf and tennis; collecting Art Deco antiques; reading and playing football with his son.

His latest pursuit is writing and this is his first self-help book.

He has lived most of his life in Norfolk, England, but has travelled extensively throughout the world and plans to continue to do so. In the past few years he has spent extensive periods of time with his family in southern Spain.

He is married to Sheryl and they have one son. Richard also has a grown up son and daughter from an earlier marriage and has three grandsons.

As one of four children himself, all of whom are in their sixties and leading active lives, this age has become a subject of which he has considerable experience and knowledge.

Since successfully selling his business in 2005 and retiring from work Richard studied, over a three year period, counselling and hypnotherapy. He is now an accredited member of The National Counselling Society and a professional member of The Hypnotherapy Society.

Whilst not actively practising these skills, studying for the qualifications has given Richard a great deal of insight into how our minds and personalities influence the way we live our lives. It has helped him to understand why some people end up with more exciting and fulfilling lives than others.

8914294R00101

Printed in Great Britain
by Amazon.co.uk, Ltd.,
Marston Gate.